BRONX BOY GOES TO WAR

I Almost Died Nine Times

Lee Evers

Bronx Boy Goes to War: I Almost Died Nine Times, by Lee Evers. Copyright © 2024 by Lee Evers. All rights reserved.

Published by Rose Press

www.rosepress.com

rosepressbooks@yahoo.com

This book may not be reproduced in whole or in part, in any form or by any means, electronic or mechanical, including recording, or by any information storage and retrieval system now known or hereafter invented, without written permission of the publisher. Brief excerpts may be quoted, in print or online, for the purpose of book reviews and articles about the book.

Cover Illustration: Lee Evers

Printed in the United States of America.

ISBN #: 978-1-7355288-0-9

Contents

Foreword by Diane Kurinsky i
Chapter 1: Born and Raised in the Bronx 1
Chapter 2: A Change of Life 6
Chapter 3: Miami Beach, Florida 10
Chapter 4: My Change of Name 13
Chapter 5: The Army Tests 15
Chapter 6: Chicago 17
Chapter 7: Chicago Error — Scott Field 19
Chapter 8: Strange Ways to Live 22
Chapter 9: Sex 23
Chapter 10: Odd Events 24
Chapter 11: Job Opportunities 26
Chapter 12: My Girlfriend 29
Chapter 13: Leaving America 33
Chapter 14: The Beach at Lae, New Guinea 35
Chapter 15: The Air Engineers 37
Chapter 16: More Odd Events 40
Chapter 17: Baseball 42
Chapter 18: Hollywood Stars 44
Chapter 19: "Pank" 45
Chapter 20: Driving 47
Chapter 21: Snakes 49
Chapter 22: Boyo's Buddy 51
Chapter 23: The Typhoon 52
Chapter 24: Me, a Military Policeman 53
Chapter 25: The Gas-Shortage Trip 54
Chapter 26: Stealing Food 56
Chapter 27: Sgt. Udelowitz 58
Chapter 28: The Radio Broadcaster 60

Chapter 29: The Piece of Shrapnel 62
Chapter 30: My Public-Speaking Class 63
Chapter 31: The All-Black Outfit 65
Chapter 32: The Movie and the Japanese Attack 67
Chapter 33: General Joe Stillwell 68
Chapter 34: Chemical Warfare 69
Chapter 35: No Promotion 71
Chapter 36: Lovely Faile 72
Chapter 37: Invitations to Move 74
Chapter 38: The Ywca in Manila 76
Chapter 39: Three-Day Celebration 77
Chapter 40: Native Villages 78
Chapter 41: Parachutists 80
Chapter 42: The Anti-Air Crafters 82
Chapter 43: No Japanese Prisoners 83
Chapter 44: Under Siege 84
Chapter 45: Anzaks 86
Chapter 46: Yellow Jaundice 87
Chapter 47: The Gold Story 89
Chapter 48: The Three-Plane Mission 91
Chapter 49: The Gay Soldier 93
Chapter 50: Captain Eckhart's Flight 95
Chapter 51: The Rubber Raft 96
Chapter 52: FDR's Death 98
Chapter 53: Guy Van 99
Chapter 54: U.S.S. Missouri 102
Chapter 55: The New Smoker 103
Chapter 56: Brownie 104
Chapter 57: The Boat Ride Home 105
Chapter 58: Mobile, Alabama 107
Chapter 59: My Dad 109
Chapter 60: Early Civilian Life 111
Chapter 61: Memories of Soldiers Past 113

So It's Over 117

FOREWORD

I first met Lee Evers in 1970. At the time, he and his wife, Lillian, were living in a one-bedroom apartment on East 15th Street in New York City. I had just begun a relationship with Lil's son David, and found myself without a place to stay while waiting to make a move to Rockland County, New York, with David and my six-month-old son, Arieh. David and I had a discussion about where we could live until we moved and he said, "We can stay with my folks for a couple of weeks, they won't mind."

"Really?" I thought. "Who doesn't mind taking a complete stranger and her baby into their house?" But David assured me that it would be no problem. And in fact both Lee and Lil did welcome us with open arms.

Although, sadly, my relationship with David didn't last, my relationship with Lee and Lil has not only lasted but has become among the most important ones in my life. Needless to say, they were a very unusual couple, and the tales of their escapades and life together could easily fill another book.

In *this* book, however, *Bronx Boy Goes to* War, Lee tells stories of his stint in the Army during World War II, after having been drafted at the ripe old age of nineteen. When I first met Lee, he was very reluctant to talk about his war experiences — in fact, it was kind of a forbidden subject. But gradually, as time went on, he began to relate some of the stories here and there. He is a great story teller. Unfettered by accuracy, he recounts the tales the way they have remained in his memory, and it seems to me the telling of these tales has served a therapeutic purpose for him over time. The stories have been a way to make sense of experiences that, as I have heard them, comprise a seminal period in Lee's life.

Imagine what it must have been like for this very sheltered Jewish boy, who had never really been anywhere out of New York City, to be thrown into the great leveling machine of the US Army. The stories in this book reveal just how much of an adjustment that was for him, and how he learned to use his many interpersonal skills, creativity, and high level of intelligence to survive a potentially terrifying and disorienting three years. Lee tells you the stories in an amusing and matter-of-fact way, often without including any commentary on his own responses except to note how strange and unusual the events seemed to him. He tells you about the many times he almost died, but does not delve into the psychological effect these experiences had on him.

I have, over the course of an almost 60-year relationship with him, drawn some conclusions as to the effect that this time in the war had on his life. As I said earlier, Lee has many gifts as a human being. He is charming, warm, funny, and smart. His social skills in large group settings seemed to grow by leaps and bounds when he found himself part of the 5th Bomber Squadron in the US Army, South Pacific. He had an easy camaraderie with his fellow soldiers and was open to suggestions for adventures when, as he writes, they were not being shot at. He is clearly an organizer and a leader, as the story about securing baseball equipment and organizing games demonstrates. He also appears to be someone interested in pleasing others and who will put aside his own plans in order to accommodate those around him.

It seems to me that although he may have started developing this style in younger years, it was honed to perfection during his time in the army. As a highly intelligent person, he quickly understood that a charming, chatty, and social person was going to have a much easier time getting by in that situation than someone who was a complainer, bad tempered, and stubborn. I often think of Lee as a Bing Crosby clone. He is smooth and easy going and cooperative on the outside, keeping his private thoughts and feelings to himself in the interest of group harmony.

I think that he also learned how to hide his fears and anxieties during his time in the Service. This must have been a really important survival skill then — how much worse it would be to be crippled by fear in those dangerous times than to adopt a matter-of-fact attitude, which maximizes action and minimizes feelings. These qualities have remained part of Lee's personality for the whole time I've known him.

Lee is also a great communicator. He mentions in one story (Chapter 4, "Mail Call") that he received more mail than any other solider in his unit. When asked why this was, he remarked that he wrote lots and lots of letters to all kinds of people. He wrote not only to his friends and family but also to politicians, manufacturing companies, and anyone he came across, either in print or in person, whom he wanted to talk to. He had, and still has, many opinions, which he is able to express clearly and well.

During the time I have known him, he has developed a vast list of birthdays of friends, family, and acquaintances to whom he sends a beautiful, hand-made collage every year on their birthday. People look forward to these cards every year and always remark on how good it makes them feel to receive them. Lee's "gift of gab," which made him popular as a soldier, also provided him with the skills needed for his long career as a salesman. To this day, people still ask him for advice about selling. His responses are clear and to the point: develop a real interest in the people you're selling to, be honest about your product and why it will be useful to them, and never try to "sell" someone on something they don't want or need. These talents helped him out in many of the situations he ran into in the Army, and they stuck with him for his whole life.

Lee's creativity and skill as a storyteller are clearly demonstrated in this book, as is his ability to create a sense of his perspective on things. He speaks often about the shift in his world from the Bronx to the South Pacific, and how that opened his eyes in many unexpected ways. He describes his ability to adapt to the different conditions he found himself in — always trying to assess and shift so as to be able to land on his feet. He also credits providence in a way that makes you understand that he's grateful for the luck he has experienced in his life and for the many friends and acquaintances who have been helpful to him along the way.

I hope you will enjoy reading this lively and charming book, and learn to love, respect, and admire the very special person who wrote it as much as I do.

Diane Kurinsky, EdD
Professor Emerita
Antioch University New England
Devoted Daughter-in-Law

CHAPTER 1

BORN AND RAISED IN THE BRONX

My wife's nephew, Donald Reiss, has repeatedly asked that I write down my war experiences. Since he's been a NASA scientist all his working life, I figured that others might also be interested in my story.

For three years, from March 1943 to February 1946, I served in the 5th Bomber Command of the United States Army during World War II and earned five battle stars. This took place in the South Pacific, including New Guinea, Moratay, three Philippine Islands, Okinowa, and many other island jungles, ending up in Japan. As I always tell people: "If it wasn't for me, you'd be speaking Japanese." I was nineteen years old when I joined the Armed Forces.

But that's not where my story starts.

It starts in New York City, on February 12, 1923, when I was born into a large Jewish family. My family consisted of my mother Anja, my father Irving, my Grandma Bubbe, my Grandfather Solomon, my Aunt Bella, and my Aunt Jennie. We lived in a very poor Jewish area surrounded by other low-income groups, including African-Americans, Italians, Irish, Polish, and Puerto Ricans.

From all accounts, I was a happy little baby. But on the week of my first birthday, my mom complained of a stomach ache. To call a doctor would have then cost a dollar (about $50 today). So she didn't get the medical care she needed, and my mother Anja died at age twenty-eight. I have no memory of her. Whenever I try to recall anything about her, I'm sadly disappointed.

As a result of my mother's death, I was raised in a rather unusual way: my closest relatives simply poured their love all over me. I was idolized. In our poor neighborhood everyone knew each other, as if it were a small village in Czechoslovakia or Poland. The moms and dads of all my friends showered me with care and warmth, simply because I was "that little boy who lost his mother."

My great fortune was having such a group of deeply caring people living with me in our large apartment house. My grandma adored me, held me, and kissed me. My lovely Aunt Bella was always around to be of help, and showered me with her love. My father, though depressed, was as attentive and loving as possible. Then there was my wonderful Zayda (*Grandpa*, in English) who owned the three-story apartment building, and was always trying to give me his attention. Lucky child was I.

My dad and my grandpa played important roles in my life. My grandfather, Sol, was an imposing man. He was very tall. Sharp grey hair bristled on his head, and his deep grey eyes looked out at you in a piercing way. He had a demanding personality and seemed stronger than anyone else I saw him with. But with me, he always smiled brightly and stroked my head.

We shared two activities; playing Dominoes and reading my father's newspaper. Grandpa would read articles to me very clearly in English, although he didn't understand a word he was reading!

I recall some quite dramatic incidences involving Zayda. In the 1920s, we had Prohibition in America but he liked his liquor, so he bought bootleg whiskey (the only way it *could* be bought). Once, two bootleggers showed up with a bottle, and Grandpa asked in Yiddish, "How much?" When they gave him the price, he firmly stated, "Too much." "OK," one replied and set a lower price. Zayda reached into his pocket, brought out a roll of bills, and handed some to the men. "That's not as much as we told you," one of the bootleggers said. Zayda stared at them, pointed his finger at the door, and the two men slunk out.

Another unforgettable incident was Zayda's response to a big dice game being played on the street in front of the apartment building. About twenty young men were rolling dice, shouting, waving their arms, and throwing coins on the street to bet or picking the coins up if they won. Zayda came running down the stairs, through the hall and past the doors, screaming out loud because he didn't want gambling in front of his building. The players picked up their coins and dashed off in all directions. I was very impressed with Zayda's power.

Now my father, on the other hand, was a handsome man. In the photos I have of him, he seems average in every way, but everyone I ever saw him with seemed to like him. Dad was a Communist and believed that Russia was the greatest nation. He attended the Communist Club, which was a block from our building. He was a bachelor after my mother's death and a sad man, and he found company and activities there, singing in the chorus and socializing with other men. I had to go to this Club almost every night to tell him dinner was ready.

Dad worked in a clothing factory in mid-town Manhattan. He always worked with a partner, and I met a number of his partners who had sons my age. These boys became my close friends.

Dad played the trumpet and the violin, but poorly, and he gave up these instruments as I grew older. With me, he played games like "roll the ball" and Tic Tac Toe. He also took me to Crotona Park field to watch soccer games, and to the swimming pool where he swam and I watched. (I was not permitted into the water, as he said it was too dangerous.) He once took me to a Catskill Mountains hotel for a week, where I was pleased to see him go off with a pretty woman on occasion. Eventually Dad remarried and started a new family, but I continued to live with my grandparents and saw him infrequently after that.

My Aunt Bella, who also lived with us, was a lovely blonde with bright blue eyes and a fetching feminine body. She was energetic and smart. She also treated me like a son. She gave me school supplies and nice clothing, and she took me with her to her job in a men's hat factory located on Greene Street in Greenwich Village. I would look out of their ninth-floor window and watch the busy street below. I clearly recall seeing the NYC police marching in unison on some special holiday from this window. I treasured Bella.

I was nine years old when my Zayda died. This was an extremely sad event and changed my life enormously. Shortly afterwards, my Aunt Bella married the man she worked for part-time in his local men's hat store, and my Dad married an unknown woman whose name was Rae. I did get to know her when I took the trolley to visit them not far away. But these two marriages on top of my Zayda's death turned my life upside down. Because instead of having many loving people around, I was now left all alone with my Bubbe.

After Zayda died, my Grandma and I lived on relief. We didn't have much money. But every Friday night she would take me to the Freeman Street movie house, where for the price of a dime they offered free food, two movies, a comedy, a newsreel, and coming attractions. Grandma would give me a penny for a chocolate bar, as well. After we got home, Grandma told whoever was around what we had seen. She was so imaginative! She combined the movies with other events and made a long story. I never got over her stories.

She also took me on five-cent bus rides to the northern tip of the Bronx and over the river to Manhattan. There, we would walk around and see what was selling at the local clothing store, then return to the bus stop, hop on the bus, and go home. As a child, I called her "Mom," believing that she *was* my mother. But as I got older, I heard my *father* call her "Mama." I figured out that she could not be mother to both of us, so I started to call her "Bubbe."

We were remarkably close. She would kiss me goodnight, glance at me with utter love in her eyes, clothe me carefully, provide foods I enjoyed, and take me with her when she went visiting or shopping. She was short, slumped slightly, and spoke only Polish and Yiddish. She *was* my mother.

I will skip now from my ninth year of age to the army experience, bypassing:

- Elementary school,
- P.S.61,
- Herman Ridder Junior High School,
- James Monroe High School,
- And the one-and-a-half years when I attended New York University's night college in Greenwich Village.

CHAPTER 2

A CHANGE OF LIFE

Luckily for me, being drafted into the Army in 1943 saved me from serious problems with the job I had at the time. I was working for a liquor wholesale company on 22nd Street and 6th Avenue in Manhattan. I learned, over the course of a year of working there, that the four owners were former gangsters/racketeers and that they admired only crookedness. While working there, I was involved in a payroll fraud. He and his friend devised a plan to skim money off the top of what the customers were paying, which brought me a lot of money. But eventually I was caught by the owners, who pondered my punishment. Fortunately, that very same week I received my draft notice, which I promptly showed them. Nodding reassuringly, they said in unison that I should go serve my country and forget everything that I had done to them. What luck! It turns out the gangsters were patriots and so they let me go without punishment.

As a matter of fact, my three years in the US Army were just full of luck. So much luck that many years later, my wife Lillian said that my mother had to be watching over me. At nineteen years old, I was provided by the war with experiences I could never have imagined.

It was Depression time, the 1930s. When I received the draft notice, I had graduated from high school and had attended one-and-a-half years of college at night at New York University while working for the liquor company. Leaving my quiet, sheltered life and going off to new cities and training camps and dealing with strange people — not to mention spending two-and-a-half years in the South Pacific — was quite a change. Even now, when I remember back to

World War II, my eyes get teary. It simply hurts to remember. Six men I knew, very young men, died in the war. I was blessed to escape death for some unknown reason, although I almost joined them on a number of occasions.

My draft notice told me to report to Grand Central Station in Manhattan at 9 a.m. on a weekday in February 1942. On that day, I bid goodbye to my Grandma and Aunt Bella, the two women who had raised me and showered me with love since my mom had died. I remember them being very matter-of-fact about it all when I left: a silent breakfast, kissing me goodbye, and waving as I left home at 8 a.m and walked down 172nd Street toward the subway station. My heart hurts as I visualize them breaking down and weeping and wailing once they could no longer see me, their precious child going off to war.

At the elevated train station on 174th Street, another surprise was waiting for me. Mrs. Warshafsky, my closest friend's mother, had come to see me off. She was a warm and caring person who took a great interest in me whenever I visited my friend, Butch. I said, "How funny it is to see you here, Mrs. Warshafsky."

She replied, "I wanted to say goodbye to you." Looking back, this also makes me want to cry.

I arrived at Grand Central Station on time. It was jammed with men in their underwear and socks standing in line, waiting for the doctors to examine them. I was directed to disrobe, given a packet of medical-report forms, and told to get on line number 1. There must have been about a dozen such lines, each with a couple of doctors in charge who would examine the men in different physical areas (such as eyes, nose, hands, feet, throat, and blood). They filled out the appropriate forms and we then went on to the next station.

At the heart station, I told the doctor about my heart murmur, which had been discovered when I was fourteen. He listened to my heart, said, "It sounds ok," and told me to do twenty push-ups. I was exhausted after that, but he listened to my heart again and said, "You're fine." I took my papers and stood on a different line.

When I finished, about two hours later, I was told to get on a final line, where I saw four military men sitting with placards in front of them on a big, long table. The signs said: "Marines," "Navy," "Merchant Marine," and "Army." From my reading the newspapers and listening to the radio, I knew that the Marines had the greatest number of casualties, since they spearheaded every battle. They were not for me. Since I did not know how to swim, the Navy and Merchant Marines were out, too. I would join the Army and be safe.

When I finally reached that long table, the officer behind the "Marines" placard looked at my papers and nodded to the other three men. This alarmed me immensely. I believed it meant that I had met their most rigorous standards and would become a Marine. "No way!" I thought. So I grabbed my papers off the table and ran back into a large crowd of draftees, hiding here and there and sneaking a look at the table from time to time. Eventually, I noticed that the Merchant Marine and the Sailor had gotten up, waved at the other men there, and left. Then the Marine left. The Army officer was the only one left collecting medical forms. So I got back on that line and was drafted into the US Army. Thank God.

From Grand Central, we got on a train that took us to Camp Upton at the far end of Long Island. I learned that it was at this base that the great song writer, Irving Berlin, composed the song, "Oh How I Hate to Get Up in the Morning." We exchanged our civilian clothes for Army uniforms, as well as shoes, gloves, a dining kit, and toiletries.

It was lunch time so I entered the mess hall, and five soldiers behind the long food table filled up my tray. I sat down with several other soldiers and examined the food. There were a number of items I had never eaten before, like bacon, ham, mashed potatoes, and unknown vegetables. I just stared at my tray, unable to imagine how I could eat this strange food. At a nearby table, I heard a voice call out: "Abe, you better get used to this food, it's all you'll ever get in the Army." I looked up and there sat a man I knew from James Monroe High School in the Bronx! His name was Jake Ellman and he had played guard on the football team. I took his advice and learned to eat the food.

After the war, we met at his large manufacturing company. I'd go in once in a while and we'd chat. Sadly, Jake died at thirty-four of a heart attack. His father and mine had worked together in NYC pressing men's pants.

CHAPTER 3

MIAMI BEACH, FLORIDA

From Camp Upton, we took a train to Miami Beach for basic training. There, I was moved into a very neat four-star hotel, where I shared a room with three other men. No explanation was given as to why we were being put up in such an expensive hotel. Each morning at 5 a.m., a Sergeant would walk through the hall shouting, "It's get-up time!" All the soldiers had to shake off sleep and quickly wash and get dressed, and then come down to the dining room, which was much fancier than anything we'd seen before as soldiers.

We ate breakfast and immediately spent an hour doing all sorts of exercises, including calisthenics. (I still do these exercises to this day, every day.) Then we were broken up into units of sixty-four men, and were taught how to march in unison. We marched hour after hour, until it was lunch time.

The drill Sergeant, Sergeant Utillo, was a tough one, and had many complaints about me. My shoe laces weren't tied tight enough, or my shirt pulled up out of my pants too much, or my turns when marching weren't as good as the other men's. Finally, it dawned on me that he was picking on me because I was the only soldier in the unit who was Jewish. My Jewishness stuck out on the dog tags that hung around my neck. Along with my name, they had a big six-pointed star that was plainly visible.

This Sergeant gave me extra duties, such as carrying bags to different places in the city (after hitching a ride on jeeps driven by soldiers), guarding certain entry areas, and washing down dirty equipment. I was perplexed and felt completely helpless. After about a week, one day a tall, heavy-set man with three Sergeant stripes on his arm came over to me in the hotel lobby. It turned out to be Lenny Joseph, a good friend from my neighborhood who had played the piano in our little band. "Hi Abie," he said.

"Len," I replied, "what are you doing here?"

"Oh," he said, "I'm assigned to a nearby base and Red" — a friend from my home neighborhood — "told me you were here, so I came to see you." We talked for about fifteen minutes and then he asked me to point out my unit leader.

"There," I pointed, "Sergeant Utillo."

Len walked over and chatted with him, then waved goodbye to me and left. And for the next three weeks, the training Sergeant never bothered me again. Lord knows what Lenny told him, but it completely changed my experience of army life.

After the war, I asked all my friends where Lenny was – I so much wanted to thank him. Sadly, no one knew, and I never saw him again.

At this point, my life seemed very strange to me, and I was extremely lonely. All the guys in my division were friendly, but being here was painfully different from my life at , where I had been surrounded by family and close friends.

It's not like there was nothing to keep up my spirits, though. All day, as we marched, there was one blond guy who would sing a variety of songs that were quite amusing, because they all involved sex. I remember one to this day:

> I used to work in Chicago
> In a big department store
> I did but I don't anymore
> A lady came in and asked for some fur
> I asked her what kind she'd adore
> Fox, she said, Fox I did
> And I don't work there anymore

Often when we were training to march military style, the leader would call out: "Onward Christian soldiers — and you too, Levine."

He knew my name was Evers. But in his mind, all Jews were Levine.

CHAPTER 4

MY CHANGE OF NAME

During that month of training, I was usually very tired. But because I longed for contact with those at home, I always wrote letters to many, many people I knew personally, including family members, friends, my girlfriend Pauline, and my colleagues at work. I also wrote letters to the Mayor of New York, my Congressman, and the two New York Senators.

Every day there was mail call. A soldier would stand up on a chair with a big packet of letters in his hand, and we would gather around him. When he called out a name, some soldier would yell out "Here" or "Yeah" or "That's me," and the mail guy would flip him a letter. I got more mail than anyone else because I wrote more letters than anyone else.

Letters came addressed to me as "Lee Evers." I had begun using that name at James Monroe High School. I was writing a gossip column for the newspaper, and my friend Moe, who ran the newspaper, said, "Ebbie, you should write a column for the newspaper like Walter Winchell."

"Okay," I said.

"But you need a different name," said Moe. "'Abraham Ebersman' is too long and clumsy."

So I figured that if I took the "man" off "Ebersmann," it would be "Ebers." And then I came up with, "Or how about 'Evers'?" That's how I got my last name.

My first name, I took from a boy in school called Lee who wore a white raincoat. And since mail was sent to me as "Lee Evers" throughout my three years in the Army, the guys all called me "Lee."

When I returned home after the war, I mentioned to my dad that I wanted to change my name legally. He said, "Sure, let's go over to City Hall." We did, I filled out some forms and signed some papers, and I was given a document that legally changed my name. I have been known as Lee Evers ever since. Thanks, Pop!

CHAPTER 5

THE ARMY TESTS

As our month of training came to an end, we had to take examinations to determine what our jobs in the Army would be. For the intelligence test, we were given a large book containing questions. When the starting bell rang, we opened it and then answered the questions on the first page. When another bell rang, we turned the page and did the same thing on that page. This went on for two-and-a-half hours. Afterwards, they gave us the results. I came in second to Gene Boyo, a guy who became a life-long friend. He got a score of 47, and I came in second with 26.

Next was the mechanical test. I was put into a very small room, about the size of a phone booth with a shelf, and given a cigar box. Sarge told me, "When the bell rings, open the box, follow the instructions on the cover of the box, and do what they say. When the bell rings again, close the lid and we'll give you another box."

The bell rang, I opened the box, and in it was a heavy metal pipe with four metal rings. The instructions were to place the rings on each side of the pipe. I tried to do it but, dang it, they did not fit! I tried and twisted them and turned them different ways, but when the bell rang I closed the lid and handed Sarge the box without having completed the task. He then gave me a second box. When the bell rang, I opened it to find a bicycle bell with a bunch of pieces. The instructions were to fit the pieces together so the bicycle bell would ring. Once again, I tried everything I could think of, but the damn thing would not ring!

Another box came after that one, along with another failure to complete the task. There must have been about twenty boxes in all.

After the test was over, all the soldiers lined up to march back to the hotel. As we were marching, a Sergeant tapped me on the shoulder, out of breath from running. "Step out of line, soldier," he ordered. When I did, he said, "You're Ebersman, right?"

"Yes, Sarge," I replied.

"Well, just so you know," he told me, "we've had about 800,000 guys take this mechanical test, and you have the lowest scores of anyone."

As I ran to catch up with my group, I thought to myself, "All right, I'm a city man and I'm not good with mechanical stuff. No big deal."

CHAPTER 6

CHICAGO

After we left Miami Beach, we all took a train to Chicago. It was a long, slow ride — the train was full of soldiers and all the other trains were higher on the military priority list, so our train was shunted aside to wait while others passed. It took three days to reach Chicago, so we all had a lot of time to talk. At night our chairs reclined, and we slept that way. For food, we walked to the Food Car and received passable portions of healthy things to eat: good high-quality, down-to-earth, simple stuff, nothing fancy — pancakes, turkey sandwiches, etc. And lots of coffee, all day long.

Luckily, I had good company. I was sitting with a guy named James O'Brien, a thirty-seven-year-old farmer from Tory, New York with seven children. "How the hell did you ever get drafted?" I asked him. Jim said that in his small community, they were required to produce a certain number of men to fulfill the draft requirement. Since they didn't have enough young or single guys, he had to go.

I was very curious about his lifestyle, which was so unfamiliar to me. His job, his wife, his seven youngsters, and his serious Catholic faith were all so different from my simple life in the Bronx. Jim, a country boy, was just as interested in my life in a New York City borough. I told him about my many family members and the numerous neighbors who fussed over me, the loss of my mom, my schooling in high school and NYU night school, my work as a reporter, my girlfriend, and my pals. It made the long train ride interesting and enjoyable.

When we got to Chicago, we were housed in the famous tall Congress Hotel. I was assigned to a room with two large bunk beds that had to accommodate four soldiers. I met two of the other three guys, who were welcoming, and we settled in. The fourth guy, a tall, heavy-set fellow, came close and fingered my dog tags with the large Jewish Star and the word "Hebrew" underneath. The guy pointed at me and started yelling, "You. You are Jewish! Oh my God — a Jew!"

I asked him, "What's wrong with you?"

"You're a devil. A Jew devil, oh my God, this is terrible — having a Jew in my room!"

The other two soldiers merely looked down at their shoes, taking no sides, while this maniac raved on and on.

I walked out the door and went along the hall until I came upon an officer. I told him what happened and requested a room transfer. "You got it, soldier," he told me, and I was sent to another room with three amicable, sensible men.

You never knew what to expect in the Army.

CHAPTER 7

CHICAGO ERROR — SCOTT FIELD

Each day, we were awakened by either a trumpet blasting or some Sergeant yelling things like, "Up and at 'em!" or "Get up, you bastards," or "Grab your socks, let go of your cocks." Then it was an hour's march around the downtown Chicago streets, breakfast in the hotel dining room, followed by an hour of gymnastics, some more marching, and a series of small group meetings about different Army subjects (e.g., weapons, weather, venereal disease).

And then it turned out that our unit had been sent to the wrong place! We were supposed to go to Scott Field, about twenty minutes from St. Louis. *God*, I thought, *this kind of error in the active war theater could have been devastating!*

So another five-hour train ride found us at Scott Field — a really nice base and, for me, a wonderful experience. Since I had been selected to be trained as a Radio Gunner, they sent me to a room full of little clickers to teach us Morse Code. We wore helmets with ear phones, and the Sergeant would click twice: two very short clicks (dot, dot) and then two longer clicks (dash, dash). Each group of clicks was a letter, and as hours passed we learned the entire alphabet.

After a few weeks, we became capable of operating as radio men and were able to handle Morse Code. Spending eight-hour days immersed in Morse Code, we became pretty proficient. Morse Code was used everywhere: on planes and boats, in tanks, etc. Having credentials as Code Operators, we would be eligible for many jobs, even after the war. I felt proud. This was a real accomplishment!

Next, we were taken to the target-practice station, where a long line of painted wooden soldier-like statues stood. We were about fifty yards away from them, with small platforms in front of us. We were given pistols, and a trainer carefully explained their parts and safety features. He told us how to aim by holding our hands way out in front of us, and how to slowly pull the trigger. We were told to fire and reload the six bullets in the pistol over and over again. Loud noises erupted all around me. My aim was fair: I hit that wooden statue in different areas. I earned a medal.

Then we were given rifles — Garands, as I recall. It was the same routine as with the pistols, but this time holding the gun to our shoulders. Next, a carbine, which was toy-like — small, slim, and lightweight. Bang, bang, bang! We learned how to insert the sixteen-shell pack into the bottom as refills.

Finally, we got Thompson Machine Guns. Boy, those were *really* weapons. I felt like a real soldier, firing those things. At lunch break, I noticed that my right ear had a ringing sound in it. *Surely it will go away soon*, I thought. Wrong. When we got aboard the bus, my ear continued to ring.

After lunch, we trudged back to our positions and were told we were to train the next group of soldiers. Sure enough, a bus arrived and out climbed black men, Negroes. One was assigned to me, and I showed him all the steps, starting with the .50 caliber pistol, the two rifles, and the machine gun. He was quick to learn and aimed well. The training ended and we got on a bus to go back. A fellow sitting next to me said, "The N's are cowards, they were scared of the guns."

"Wait a minute," I interjected, "my guy did as well as any of our men. You're talking crazy."

He looked down and said nothing else.

At the mess table, my buddy Gene Boyo sat next to me. "Gene," I told him, "my ear is ringing. Is yours?"

"Hell no, Evers."

"If it doesn't stop, I'm going to the medical section."

"Yeah," Gene said, "you want to get a discharge paper."

Well, the next morning my ear kept ringing. I told the Sergeant I had to see an ear doctor, and he gave me a pass. At the medical station, a Lieutenant heard my story, looked into my right ear with a glass piece of some kind, grunted, and took a soft white stick with a piece of cotton on the end and stuck it in my ear.

"Hmm," he said. "Does it still ring?"

"Yes," I told him.

The Lieutenant called out for the Captain to come to his station. The Captain came, took a small wooden stick and placed a piece of cotton on the end, and stuck it into one of my nostrils. "The ringing stop, soldier?"

"No, sir," I said.

The Captain stepped into the hallway and told a passing solider to get the Major. The Major listened to what the Lieutenant and the Captain told him, took a wire, place a piece of cotton on the end, put it in my nostril, and pushed it way up. "Feel any better?" he inquired.

"No sir, my ear is still ringing," I said.

The Colonel was called in. I was told that he was a leading ear specialist. He listened to all the reports of my examinations, then just looked at me and finally said, "Soldier, you'll just have to live with this condition. It's part of being in the Army."

Seventy-five years later, that darn ear is still ringing! The VA finally gave me hearing aids when I was ninety-two years old.

CHAPTER 8

STRANGE WAYS TO LIVE

The oddest part of being in the Army was being told to do an amazing number of things I had never done before, like wearing the heavy boots they issued me, and sleeping on a cot or small bed. You had to make the bed with sheets stretched so tight that the officer who inspected it could drop a quarter on it and have it bounce. If it did not bounce, the bed had to be made all over again.

Another strange thing was having to share a bathroom with so many other guys. The bunks usually had long metal basins stretched across the room, and we would line up and urinate together.

There were also numerous maintenance chores to be done, like washing the barracks windows. Wow! High up on a thin ladder you'd go, and have to lean over to do this job. Scary work! For the floors, you were given a small brush and bucket and you would slowly wash down the dirty floor on your hands and knees. You had to get up to wash out the brush many times.

Then there was KP — Kitchen Patrol. In the mess hall, you'd be assigned to wash the pots. They were huge, big as garbage cans. You had to use a big brush, run boiling water, and scrub hard.

It was really difficult to do and you worked up a big sweat.

These, and so many other strange, new activities were asked of me. I entered the Army at the young age of nineteen, and due to many harsh experiences left three years later, feeling about forty-six. Being in the Army really matured me and enabled me to handle any other difficulties in my life quite easily after that.

CHAPTER 9

SEX

The Scott Field Army base was about twenty minutes outside St. Louis. Whenever we had Radio-Gunnery training, we'd hitch a ride into that city or nearby small towns. One night, when I was in town with my friend Irving Sprechman, we ran into a woman of about forty named Eileen Morris. She was quite friendly, and at the end of the car ride she let each of us enjoy sex with her. I've always wondered how she could be so casual about such an important act.

Another time, I was with Gene Boyo when we met three middle-aged women. One of them, who was married and owned a beauty salon, invited us to go for a ride in her car. I sat next to her in the middle of the front seat and was able to fondle her as she drove. Her friend, who sat on my other side, was quiet and distant. In the back seat, Gene was busy engaging in the sex act with the third woman, who sprawled over him as he slunk down in the seat, and was actively pumping up and down until she moaned. When we reached the bar, two of the women and Gene got out. Then the driver and I got into the back seat and enjoyed a quickie.

A few weeks later, after Gene had shipped out, I was called to the phone in our barracks. A woman asked me if she could talk to Gene.

"Sorry," I told her, "he's gone."

"Oh," she murmured, "I'm pregnant and he won't know about it."

"Gee," I said, "if I hear from him, I'll tell him."

Months later, I informed him of this call in a letter. Although Gene and I remained friends for sixty more years, we never referred to this experience again.

CHAPTER 10

ODD EVENTS

On another occasion, Gene Boyo and I were in a bar in St. Louis having a beer. Three rough-looking sailors came in, sat nearby, and gazed at us. They looked angry, like they were ready to attack anyone who stared back. "Gene," I said, "let's get out of here, those guys are looking for a fight." So I left money on the bar and we hastened out. We were no match for these guys.

One of the strangest things was being in a training session learning how to attack an enemy stronghold. The "enemy" was holed up, and as we crept along toward their outpost, a paper "hand grenade" landed at my side. Boyo leapt up, grabbed it, and lobbed it back to the enemy line. Then he said to me, "Now that I've saved your life, Evers, you owe me for as long as you live." Oddly enough, we met again in New York City after the war and became steadfast friends, did a huge number of fun things together with our families, and were friends until the day he died. He was a wonderful guy. I owed him "my life." I did name my only biological child, Gene, after him.

Life at Scott Field was good, but I was still very lonely. On Christmas night, I was lying on top of my bunk listening to Bing Crosby sing "White Christmas." I felt so utterly lonely — missing my Grandma, Aunt Bella, Cousin May, and all my pals — that I began to cry, and I cried for a long time. It was one of the saddest days of my life.

Still, the interesting, exciting, and unusual experiences I was having distracted me and forced me to open my eyes to so many different ways of life than the smaller world I had known in the Bronx.

Sometimes it was hard for me to understand how or why these things happened to me, and sometimes it was just amusing to be part of things I never would have imagined.

Once, in a huge auditorium in St. Louis, a medical Colonel was giving a speech about avoiding venereal disease. There were about 1,500 soldiers in the hall, and a Captain was walking up and down the aisle searching for faces. He finally leaned over me and told me to get up and go to the stage to assist the Colonel. I did as I was told. But I still don't know why he picked me out of so many.

On Thanksgiving, my friend John Antonelli had been invited to a deaf woman's home for dinner and he asked me to come along. It was such a strange experience, since she could not talk, but she gladly fed us a delicious turkey dinner with all the fixings.

Every Sunday of the six weeks we spent at Scott's Field, Jimmy O'Brien (the thirty-seven-year-old guy I had met on the train) awakened me early and told me to get dressed because I was going to church with him.

"Jim," I told him, "I'm Jewish."

"So what?" he'd ask. "Just sit in the back and listen."

I really appreciated the lovely religious services, and to this day I clearly recall how deeply touched I was by all the people praying.

Things could go easily from one extreme to the other. One day I was in church with my Catholic friend, and another day at chow a large man opposite me saw my dog tags and called me a "dumb Jew." He was so big that I couldn't possibly handle him, but at the end of the table an equally big guy with a mustache told him to "back off or deal with me." The nuisance left our table.

Another time, Gene Boyo, who worked with the public relations people at Scott Field, set up a dance and invited college women. He wanted to get a big crowd. I drew colorful pictures of large-breasted women dancing and hung them on all the barracks' bulletin boards. The dance was a huge success and Gene Boyo couldn't praise me enough.

CHAPTER 11

JOB OPPORTUNITIES

When it came time to be assigned our future work in the Army, my unusual experiences continued. First, my radio instructor told me I was so smart that he could get me a job as an instructor like him. Unfortunately I had to refuse the kindly offer, since I knew I totally lacked any mechanical ability. If I'd been able to accept, I would have avoided going overseas for almost three years.

The reason the instructor thought I was so smart was that since the radio was a complete mystery to me, I had memorized where the wires went, what the knob positions were, how to operate the antenna, and the radio instruction booklet. In this way, I could successfully operate that radio while being completely unable to understand its inner workings.

The next amazing thing happened when I was picked for Pilot training. Wow! This meant I'd be a flyer, an officer. I wouldn't have to do any of the hard soldier-stuff. I'd be a lieutenant, pilot a plane, and earn decent money. Only four men out of the sixty-four in our company were selected to be pilots. I was elated. What good luck! I immediately wrote a letter to my Aunt Bella, who was able to read English, and asked her to also tell my Grandma this wonderful news.

The next day, I was picked up by jeep and driven to a nearby small airport. I was met by a short, red-haired soldier named Sgt. Dean. He told me to get into a tiny airplane, which I learned was a Piper Cub. I sat just behind him, squeezed in with very little room, and Sgt. Dean started the engine. I was fascinated by the wooden propeller, which slowly began to rotate and spin faster and faster. As the Piper

Cub started down the runway, I could still make out the spinning propeller. Sgt. Dean explained the different terms pilots used for take-offs, landings, turns, weather conditions, and all kinds of other things necessary to fly a plane. He circled St. Louis at a low level, telling me to radio the tower. There was a small shelf on my left side with a radio sitting on it. I picked up the headphones, pushed the familiar button, and above a crackling noise heard a voice announce: "Scott Field Military." I responded as trained: "This is Pvt. Abraham Ebersman reporting from Training Flight #1107 with Sgt. Dean piloting our craft." Then the crackling voice said, "Received. Over and out."

Each day for about a week, I flew over St. Louis with Sgt. Dean. In his Mississippi drawl, he would tell me to do different things, like report to him on the weather, tell him how many vehicles I could count on the ground, and another time to ask "ground" what the expected weather conditions were for the next day. At mail call toward the end of the week, I had a letter from my Aunt Bella. She wrote me, "Don't You Dare Be a Pilot. You could get killed! Grandma also agrees."

What the hell should I do, I wondered. Aunt Bella and my Grandma were my parents. They had raised me and done everything for me. There was no way I could ignore their wishes.

The next morning, instead of going to train with Sgt. Dean in the Piper Cub I went to Headquarters, where a blond Major was sitting. "Yes, soldier, what can I do for you?" he asked.

"Well, sir, I was selected for pilot training and Sgt. Dean has been flying me all over for the last few days, but I just received a letter from the people who raised me. Here it is, sir." I handed him the letter.

"Jesus!" the Major shouted, and looked up at me. "You want to quit the flying school?"

"Yes sir, I have no choice."

"Christ, this is really shit," he said. He took the application papers I was holding, spread them out on his desk, took a rubber stamp, pressed it down on a large ink pad, and stamped all the papers "AIR SICK." I assume that he decided to justify my quitting in this way because he had no standard explanation for his superiors that involved a letter from my family.

Oddly, in spite of the "AIR SICK" stamp all over my papers, when we were assigned work positions I was told I would be part of Radio Gunnery and be part of a bomber crew.

Me — Air Sick?

CHAPTER 12

MY GIRLFRIEND

One Friday afternoon, I was informed that a woman was waiting for me at Headquarters. When I arrived, to my utter surprise there was Pauline — my girlfriend from the Bronx. Since our relationship hadn't been very serious, I called out, "Hey, what the heck are you doing here?"

She said, "I wanted to see you before you went overseas. Your letters kept me up-to-date on what was going on, so I took the train to St. Louis and a cab from there to here."

It was shocking. Totally unexpected. I could not come to grips with Pauline being here, all alone, far from home, and me really unable to be of much help in terms of where she would sleep, or what to do with her while she was here. The officer in charge of the base was sitting behind a desk. I turned to him and explained that I had the weekend off and my girlfriend had made a long trip to see me. I asked if I could be excused from the base for the weekend. He entered information on a pad and told me to report back Monday morning by 8 a.m. I thanked him, took Pauline's hand, and we got on the bus to St. Louis.

I was very confused by her being here, and listened only half-heartedly as she told me about her job in lower Manhattan, her mother, father, relatives, and girlfriends. Finally arriving in St. Louis, we passed a YMCA. I pulled the cord, the bus stopped, and we got off. Inside the "Y" a band was playing and a huge group of soldiers were dancing.

Pauline and I sat down in a nearby empty room. I looked at her. As usual, she was very pretty, shapely, dark-haired with soft brown eyes. My thinking went this way: "She came here alone to be with me. I have few resources. She wants to spend a week of her vacation time here, and I cannot send her back to the Bronx where everyone she knows will know we've been together." So I said, "Pauline, will you marry me?"

She smiled lovingly and said, "Of course I will." After all, I was almost twenty years old, a man, a soldier. So in case I got killed, she'd receive whatever a wife receives in such cases.

We walked over to the Main Office, where a woman was sitting behind a desk. "Ma'am," I told her, "my girlfriend just arrived from New York and we want to get married."

She asked us how old we were and our religion.

"I'm nineteen," I said, and Pauline gave her age. "We're Jewish," I added.

"All right," the woman said, "I'll contact a Rabbi, who will handle all the legal matters. Hold on while I phone him." After some time talking on the phone, she turned to us and said, "The Rabbi is vacationing in the mountains nearby and is going to drive back to his home to marry you. I'll arrange for one of our drivers to take you there." A fellow in civilian clothing came to the door and told us to meet him out back.

So Pauline and I, holding hands, strolled past all the dancing couples toward the rear door of the YMCA. The music stopped and a voice came over the loudspeaker: "A couple from New York are getting married. One is a soldier from Scott Field. Anyone interested can follow our 'Y' car in the parking lot out back." Pauline and I got into the waiting car, and it backed out of our space and turned towards the busy main street. To my surprise, other cars were following us. They began to blow their horns, and their passengers waved their hands to people on the streets. It was a long ride to the Rabbi's house, which turned out to be quite large and have a big parking area. All the cars following us parked there, about a dozen of them, and all the people packed into the Rabbi's living room.

The Rabbi smiled at everyone. He was an elderly man with a big hat. His wife got a big cloth, which was stretched out over our heads, and he then read off the marriage ceremony. We signed some papers, and everyone was given a glass of wine. Many congratulated us. We were married.

One tallish man, Maurice, said to me, "Solider, I've reserved a room for you at the best hotel in town. When you're ready, I'll drive you there." That night, my new wife, Pauline, and I slept in a first-class room. But Pauline was very cold and distant. She was raised in a family where the parents didn't like each other and so she never learned how to be affectionate. She was very smart — she had graduated high school at the age of fifteen and gotten a scholarship to college. But she was standoffish with me, because she was not interested in a romantic relationship.

The next day, we had a free breakfast and walked around St. Louis. When we got back to the hotel, Maurice was waiting. He told me he was taking us to his home to spend the weekend with his family. It turned out that Maurice owned a fluorescent-light company, had a lovely home with a swimming pool, a pretty wife, Ellen, and two little kids, a boy and a girl. I'll never forget this unexpected kindness. We were so lucky.

I was unsure how my new wife would spend the rest of her week, since I had to be back at the base, but my friend Jim O'Brien told me he had rented a room at a nearby farm for *his* wife, who wouldn't be arriving until a few days later. Pauline and I got a ride to the farm, where the farmer, dressed in typical farmer's clothing, told me, "Sure, your wife can stay until Jim's wife shows up. It's already paid for." I hung around a while as Pauline settled in. Hearing the farmer talk was like listening to a movie, unbelievable to a city boy like me. It was real country talk. I had to stifle my laughter.

So Pauline stayed at the farmhouse for the rest of her week. During the entire period, we never touched, kissed, or did anything sexual. I didn't think of myself as being married. It was in name only.

CHAPTER 13

LEAVING AMERICA

After Pauline left to go back to the Bronx, my squadron was sent from St. Louis to Pittsburgh, California, near San Francisco. It was a way station for us on our trip overseas. A couple of days after arriving, I was awakened around 2 a.m. by a Sergeant holding a dim red lamp. "Follow me," he ordered. I got into a pair of pants, shoes, and jacket, and walked with him to join a group of soldiers who were yawning and rubbing their eyes, just like me. We were marched out of the barracks to a large, empty field. They had the thirty of us sit in a large circle, and an officer stood in the center. I noticed that a large truck had pulled up nearby.

"Men," the officer announced, "here are the various pieces of fighting equipment you'll soon need." Each man was issued a large furry hat, heavy gloves, thick socks, tough-feeling underwear, pants, shirts, and everything necessary to survive in the Arctic. "We must be going to Alaska," I told the guy next to me. Finally we each got a big green duffle bag and were ordered to put our stuff into it, tie the cords, and tell no one about this matter.

The next afternoon, we were trucked to a train, which took us to San Francisco. We got off on a big pier and were instructed to be very quiet, since this was a secret operation. In the middle of the night, we began to walk up a large ship's gangplank, carrying the duffle bags on our shoulders. I realized that this ship would be taking us to our next station and that secrecy was important so the Japanese submarines in the Pacific did not attack our ship. As I trudged up the gangplank, with dawn breaking, I heard a very loud noise: a huge band was playing a military song, but loud! Then I saw a vast crowd of people standing all over the pier, waving American flags and shouting, yelling, screaming all sorts of good wishes, and wishing us luck. What a send-off! How would the Japanese subs react? I wondered.

The boat was huge, and had an Italian name. It moved smoothly, and calmly proceeded over the huge Pacific Ocean. Everything was very orderly. We'd line up for each meal and eat it standing at an upright pole with a flat board on it so you could put your mess kit and coffee cup on it. I did get seasick for the first day, but then it passed.

After six days, we came to a port in southern New Guinea called Lae. "Hmm," I mused, "what about the cold-weather clothing and equipment we were given?" I guessed it was done to mislead any possible enemy spies who might have been around the Pittsburgh base.

CHAPTER 14

THE BEACH AT LAE, NEW GUINEA

My outfit was lined up on the sandy, sunny beach. A Major walked up and down the line, explaining the situation. He proclaimed, "You hundred guys are assigned to ten B-24s. Each plane had a crew of ten men: pilot, co-pilot, engineer bombardier, cartographer, belly, tail, front and side gunner, and a radio gunner for the other side. Well, the bad news is that the Japanese were on this island and closed the Owen-Stanley Mountains. We were ordered by MacArthur's section to attack. The ten empty planes that were waiting at the airport were without crews, so we dug up troopers to fly them and attack the Japanese. After we beat them back, we were ordered to leave the makeshift crews intact, so you guys have no jobs."

As a result of this, when we landed at Lae, a tiny town, we were told we had been assigned to the Fifth Bomber Command. The Fifth Bomber Command had General Ulysses S. White, a graduate of West Point, as its commander. We were part of the forces sent to the South Pacific to stave off further advances by the Japanese Army and Navy, which had successfully overrun huge areas of China and all of the nearby island nations, such as Borneo, the Philippines, Indonesia, and Taiwan. They also took over dozens of small island groups like Guam, Iwo Jima, the Marshal Islands, Midway, and many others.

As we stood at attention that day, different officers roamed our line and selected men for all kinds of work that was needed. Some became mechanics or radio repairmen. Others were electrical workers or carpenters. A Colonel came up to me and said, "I see you know how to type and you held a responsible sales job."

"Yessir," I saluted.

"Well, my top Sarge was sent back to Minneapolis with an injury and I need someone like you to do my work. Show up tomorrow at the Air Engineers."

I saluted again, and went back on a truck to a newly developed open patch in the vast jungle. Three other guys were setting up a tent and asked me to join them. I'll never forget Bill Primavera from Cranston, Rhode Island; Vic Clodin from the Bronx; and John Morlino from Upper Darby, PA. We stayed together throughout the war, and I kept in touch with Vic afterwards. I had never lived in a tent before and it required a lot of adjusting.

Of course, living in a jungle also made for a lot of strange adjustments. It was far from the Bronx! Whenever you had to urinate, you'd walk into the nearby woods and do it. To defecate outdoors, there were twelve holes cut into a square section of wood and you'd squat down alongside other men to do it. As for showering, you'd step into a cubicle with a hose handle overhead. Soon, warm water covered your body. Then the water stopped and you soaped your body. The water came on for a few more minutes after that. This way, scarce water would not be wasted. At the end, you'd step out of the cubicle and dry yourself.

There were two seasons in New Guinea: Summer and Rain. We were in the Summer one and it was hot — very hot. It was over 100 degrees every day. We wore only our boots, shorts, and helmet. We always carried a weapon and a water canteen. At night I found the cot okay to sleep on but had to use mosquito netting to avoid bites. One electric bulb was attached to the center tent-pole so we could sit around, play cards, read, or talk about civilian life.

We four did become good friends. The Fifth Bomber Command did a variety of things in addition to dropping bombs. For example, John worked as a five-stripe Sergeant for the chemical warfare section. Billy, a Corporal, handled postal services, and Vic did all kinds of surveying in the Engineer section.

CHAPTER 15

THE AIR ENGINEERS

The next day, after settling in with my new tentmates, I reported to the Air Engineer's office — a tent with a small wooden desk, a typewriter, and a phone. A Captain, Major, and Colonel were there, and the Colonel gave me a number of tasks. I learned that the "Air Engineers" was not a real division but had been created to fill vital needs for the war effort that no one else was assigned to handle. The Colonel wanted me to type up a daily activity list for whatever we had done that day. He asked me to read the secret intelligence reports and brief him on the important matters disclosed. I was also to keep track of all cargo ships that arrived at the Lae port, and get their captain's names and the nature of the cargo that got unloaded.

All day long, a variety of officers came in asking for assistance with a variety of different needs. These included securing trucks for deliveries or pick-ups and securing jeeps for different trips, and obtaining materials such as cement, wires, and so many other items. They also included securing natives to do certain work. The Colonel's name was Herbert Imb, from Easton, PA. The natives were short, Black, and strong as can be imagined. They would come to the camp nude, carrying spears, wooden clubs, and bows and arrows. We had their Australian overseers put them to work for us, paying them very little. They cut trees, carried lumber, cleaned up, and whatever other tough jobs we needed, they did them. I also recall them unloading trucks, loading up airplanes, and carrying huge containers.

Eventually, we moved from southern Lae to a northern area called Leyte (lay-tay). The first time I walked into our camp area, two

Japanese fighter planes flew over us, splattering the area with machine-gun fire. As trained, I threw myself on the ground, hands over my head. The planes passed, and we got up and resumed what we were doing. The next day, the same thing happened — machine-gun fire as a couple of Japanese planes shot by. Boy, it was scary!

The native workers were unloading ships at the pier and cleaning up messy areas. I've always believed that these natives were badly mistreated. The Australians should have set up schools and hospitals and encouraged them to have their own businesses.

Working for the Colonel in New Guinea seemed like it would be a good thing. As part of the 5th Bomber Command, the "Air Engineers" were vital. All materials that arrived by ship or air were channeled through us. General Douglas MacArthur appointed our General White to destroy the Japanese military might.

My own experiences continued to be utterly strange to me. My tentmates all held different jobs, but we got up around the same time. We'd walk to the Mess Tent, where a bunch of wooden tables were set up with long benches. The cooks would serve us pancakes and bacon and bread for breakfast as well as hard-boiled eggs, sometimes. The coffee was endless. Wherever we were, a coffee cart or a coffee canister was handy so we could have coffee. And cigarettes! They were free and given to us plentifully in carton form. Of course, this didn't mean too much for me because I did not smoke.

Whenever a holiday came up and we were not in some kind of combat or danger, I'd tell my office that I would take over a kitchen police spot for a Christian soldier so that they could enjoy Christmas or Easter or whatever. My first day on K.P. in New Guinea, I entered the kitchen area and found five rather big men there. It turned out they also were Jewish. They picked me up and held me up in the air, marched around the Mess, and used Yiddish words to congratulate me upon being a volunteer. Now, how many guys would get such treatment?

One oddity I never got over was the way the guys talked while we ate. All the language was as coarse as could be imagined. Everyone seemed to use curse words, and the dirtier they were, the more often I heard them. It really astounded my ears and I never really got over it. I guess it was a sort of release for pent-up feelings most of the guys carried around.

CHAPTER 16

MORE ODD EVENTS

I have never forgotten the day a huge supply plane was landing, and I had to be there to handle the paperwork. Seated on the grass were about forty natives in a long line. As the plane was unloaded, small items were carried out by hand, but the huge tank and jeep parts were unloaded by a motorized metal platform on wheels. The parts were then taken to a large wooden stall, where they were put together on assembly lines manned by trained mechanics. At the end of the line, a completed jeep or tank would emerge! It was incredible to watch. I was standing next to an Australian soldier who worked with the natives, since his country "owned" New Guinea. He told me: "These natives believe your plane was sent here by God. They can't figure out how such big ships fly and how pieces of metal, rubber, wood and wires end up as jeeps and tanks."

One lunch period, as we walked towards the Mess Hall with some soldiers, we passed a Black engineer barracks and a record was playing. It was a beautiful melody, and a fantastic woman's voice was singing "Traveling Light." I stopped to listen — I loved it and couldn't believe any song could be that lovely. I turned to a couple of Black troopers and asked, "Say, who is that singing?"

"Man, that's Billie Holiday. She's cool," was the reply.

Hearing that, a bell went off in my head. A year before being drafted, I was attending NYU night college in Greenwich Village three nights a week. I walked past a small nightclub with a large poster in front that had the face of a pretty woman with a white flower over one ear. It was Billie Holiday. I passed that poster over and over, always regretting that I could not afford to buy a drink and see her. It still feels like a big loss in my life. After that, she was barred from New York City for her drug use.

One of the officers hanging around my "office" was a Captain Kritzman from Kansas. He told a group of us a story one day that I've never forgotten. As he explained it, a fairly large group of married couples would meet in a different home every Saturday night, have drinks, and listen and dance to music from the radio and kid around. They agreed, at one such get-together, to place sets of keys to their homes on a table top. Then, each woman would go up to the table and select a set of keys. The man who owned the set of keys would go home with the woman and stay overnight. I was shocked! Yet the other officers present thought it was a fun way to behave.

One day, I was working in the fields with a group of men. Among them was a pleasant guy from the Chicago area named Snead. Always friendly, he joined me in a game of cards one night, and hastened to my table when he saw me in the Mess Tent. I enjoyed him. Snead got really drunk one night when one guy opened a large bottle of scotch, and started to rant about "the fucking Jews." I was appalled, although the other men shrugged him off. After that incident, I never spoke to Snead again. He kept after me asking over and over why I was angry with him. It's a sad memory for me.

CHAPTER 17

BASEBALL

Our forces had already chased the Japanese off the Southern area of New Guinea when I arrived in Lae, so things were quiet, thank God. After about a month, there was very little time I spent there without danger of some sort.

About a week after arriving, as I looked out at the water I saw a ship being unloaded and sporting equipment being piled up. I asked the officer in change how my outfit could get some baseball bats and gloves. "Fill out the request form," he said, and handed me a sheet of paper. Back in my "office" (just a small chair and a shaky desk), I typed in the necessary information on the request form. Sure enough, a few days later, a big box was delivered to the Colonel's area with my name on it. In it was all the equipment necessary for a bunch of baseball teams.

I drew up a neat bulletin about this, stating that interested soldiers should contact me. Then I made copies and placed them on bulletin boards around our camp. Sure enough, soon a bunch of soldiers came over to my tent wanting to play baseball.

I took down their names and tent numbers, set up four teams, and informed everyone. Some were electrical people, some were carpenters, still others were plane mechanics, and my team was the Air Engineers. I set up a game schedule and invited officers to be the umpires, and for a couple of weeks, games were played when it was feasible — that is, when the Japanese were not attacking us, strafing us from planes, sharp shooters in the trees, and heavy planes containing bombs. I kept records of the games and posted them on bulletin boards so that anyone who cared could see the scores, pitchers' names, home-run hitters, etc. It was a fun time.

A month later, the trouble began, and after that we had no peace and quiet. Two-and-a-half years of murder.

In one game we played, an opposing player ran from third base to the plate and knocked my catcher down. I ran out to the umpire to complain that it was an "out." The umpire, a Lieutenant, was uncertain, and to make things worse, the other team had a brute called Mays who threatened me. So I backed off.

I've often since thought with regret about my weakness at that time. I should have gone to my tent, gotten my carbine, and *then* argued with Mays, so that his size would not have intimidated me.

CHAPTER 18

HOLLYWOOD STARS

During one of our games, a famous Hollywood actor appeared. It was Joe E. Brown — a comedian and actor from the 1930s and '40s. "Hey fellers," he called out. Someone in our troop saw him, recognized his familiar face, and ran over. "Look," Joe E. explained, "I'll be going back to the States soon, so if any of you want me to contact someone back in the U.S., tell me and I'll phone them, tell them I met you here, and that you're ok and whatever else you want me to say." So for about an hour, this guy wrote down the names and phone numbers of folks back home for Joe E. Brown to contact. Later, I learned from several men that he had spoken to their families, who were touched by his kindness. I also learned that his son had been killed fighting in Italy, so he did this in part to deal with his loss.

Another Hollywood star, John Wayne, also showed up. I was waiting on the mess line, holding my metal tray, and looked up to see John Wayne standing there serving food. He smiled and piled some food on my tray. I was shocked — John Wayne serving food to troops in the New Guinea jungles! My tentmate, John Marlino, was charged with driving Wayne to nearby encampments, where the actor would partake in ordinary activities so soldiers would feel more of a connection with him. When John returned that evening, we all questioned him. "What is he like?" "What did he tell you about making movies?" "Did he talk about women?" John told us that Wayne didn't say anything worth repeating, but that whatever he said, he used the filthiest language you can imagine. Every other word was a curse word. "What a creepy man," he said.

CHAPTER 19

"PANK"

A couple of days later, I saw three women in Salvation Army duds pushing a wooden contraption on four wheels that had a huge coffee urn and sticks holding donuts. "Say, soldier, do you want coffee and a donut?" they asked me.

"Sure," I told them, "but you shouldn't be here. We get shot at by Japanese planes regularly. Go find a safe area to offer these treats." Nevertheless, several of us stood and talked with them. Women were a rare sight in these parts.

Later on, when I had been home from the war for one week, my buddy Moe got me a job with an outstanding wrought-iron-furniture company on 72nd Street and East Side Drive in Manhattan. As I was being taken around their five-floor firm and introduced to the higher officials, I noticed that one woman looked familiar. I wracked my brain and finally remembered her. She was one of those three women offering coffee and doughnuts near Leyte, New Guinea!

"Hey," I said to her, "you were in the war, a Salvation Army woman, right?"

She was surprised. "You know me?"

"Yes, I remember you were with two others, and I told you to go elsewhere because this area was being strafed often and you would be an easy target."

"Oh yes," she replied, and told me that her name was Pank Flansburgh. We worked together for the year-and-a half I stayed with this furniture house, until I quit because the General Manager and I got into a dispute.

Fortunately, I soon connected with a small toy-manufacturing outfit on 23rd Street and 5th Avenue, the world center for toys, and was appointed office manager of their fifth-floor display office. One day, as I was walking along the seventh floor for some reason, I passed an office with an open door — and there was Pank, typing away. Of course, after that we met several times to enjoy lunch and conversation with each other.

Many years later, when I was living in Stuyvesant Town apartments in Manhattan, Pank turned up again, living on the ninth floor of my own building. She later moved, but I bumped into her yet again when I attended a friend's party on 32nd street. From then on, my wife and I would meet her for coffee or dinner for many years.

One day, she told me that she was moving to a small Caribbean Island to be with her nephews. I lost track of her for a few years, and then I got a phone call from her nephew saying that she had passed away. She was quite a bit older than my wife and me, but still relatively young.

About three years later, I received a phone call from some Army branch asking me if I knew someone called "Alide Flansburgh."

"Sure," I said, "we called her 'Pank.' What do you want to know?"

"Sir," said the voice on the other end of the phone, "we understand that she served for the Salvation Army in World War Two. Can you confirm that?"

"Oh, yes. She was in the front lines in Leyte, New Guinea. A very brave woman."

"All right sir," the caller said, "her name will be included on the Washington DC Monument dedicated to women who served in the war."

CHAPTER 20

DRIVING

Colonel Imb was hardly ever around. He would just sign a packet of notes and then leave me in charge. I would hand out these notes to the officers and higher Sergeants who needed different supplies to accomplish their tasks. For example, someone would say: "I need four trucks, twenty natives and two G.I.s to finish the bridge over the river," or "Gotta have two jeeps and drivers to get the oil cans to the airport," or "Must get a release form for a propeller to replace a broken one." And so on.

One morning, the Colonel told me to deliver a heavy envelope to General White's office: "Get the jeep and get this package to his orderly."

"Colonel," I said, "I don't know how to drive a jeep." I had never even driven a car in New York.

"Well fuck it, learn how to drive and deliver this. Now!"

So I walked out of the tent/office and stood looking at the jeep, holding the envelope. A soldier walked by. "Hey feller," I called, "can you show me how to drive this thing?"

He scratched his head. "You don't know how to drive?"

I shook my head sadly.

He had me sit in the driver's seat. "See this?" he instructed. "It's the key. Turn it and the motor starts. This is the brake. Release it like this. And there's three speeds: first, second, and third. It determines how fast you'll drive. Put your foot on the brake to slow down or stop. Good luck." And with that, he walked off.

I did what he said. I drove very slow in first gear through the jungle path to General White's office. When I got there, I handed the packet to his orderly, who signed my receipt, and then I returned to where I had parked the jeep — on a hill, facing an area that fell off sharply. Since I was new at driving, I was afraid that if I was clumsy starting up the jeep, it might move forward and fall over the cliff. So when a soldier walked by, I asked him if he would back my jeep off the parking spot for me. He was happy to do it, but looked as me strangely as I climbed in.

See, I was a quick learner. And also very, very, careful.

CHAPTER 21

SNAKES

Talk about a Bronx youth landing on an island far from home called Moratai! When our small landing crafts were pulled up on the beach, we got out carrying our duffle bags with all we owned in them, ready to settle into a new jungle camp. But instead we were told to line up, and a jeep drove past us. The driver reached into the back for a large, rounded knife called a machete.

"Men," the Major called out, "you will need these to cut off the heads of the many poisonous snakes that are all over the island. So be careful, look everywhere, and kill the bastards." It was a frightening few days until we did kill many snakes and could stop looking sharply around all day. The Bronx was never like this.

Speaking of snakes, here's where I set the international record for the fifty-yard dash. After having a tough day dealing with a Japanese episode of some consequences, I was chatting with a couple of guys late at night when the Colonel came by, holding a bottle of Scotch. "Evers," he said to me, "you and these men did a good job and deserve this Scotch." "These men" were Jorgenson, a Swede from upper Michigan, and Sundstrom, a Norwegian from North Dakota.

They were trained mechanics who repaired pipes, wheels, and electrical things, and used a small shed to store the materials they used for their work. Jorgenson pointed to this shed and suggested that we go there to enjoy the Scotch.

It was dark as we trudged up a slight hill and got to the shed. Sundstrom took keys out of his pocket and used them to unlock the doors. It was really dark inside the shed. Jorgensen called out, "Evers, there's a cord hanging down in front of you. Pull it and the light will come on." So I reached up, and sure enough there was thick cord hanging there. I pulled it down and the light lit up the shed. I was holding the neck of flat-headed snake, its fangs erupting from its mouth.

I gaped at it. I gasped. I nearly had heart failure. I dropped the snake and dashed out of the shed and raced down the slight hill. Boy, did I run fast! I was lightning itself! Anything to get away from that horror.

When I finally stopped the fifty-yard dash, I heard Sundstrom calling, "Evers, come back. We killed the fucker." So I climbed back up the hill.

But I'm utterly convinced that no human could run as fast as I did, trying to get away from that ugly reptile because of how scared I was.

CHAPTER 22

BOYO'S BUDDY

My buddy Gene Boyo was serving in India, and one day I got a letter from him telling me about all kinds of intriguing things he was experiencing. Near the end of the letter, he asked me to go visit a college friend of his who was on a small island nearby. He thought this guy and I could become friends. He asked me to update his friend about Gene's activities and, of course, our past fun times.

We had one day a week off when not in some kind of combat. So I borrowed a jeep from Bernie Schursky, the Motor Pool manager, and drove to the pier facing the island Gene had mentioned. Seeing an officer at a tent nearby, I explained why I needed a vessel to take me over to the island.

"Soldier," he said very slowly, "we sent 700 troops over there a week ago. They were supposed to cut down trees to get wood to build a camp, but we got word that there was some kind of infestation, probably bugs or lice or something. All those poor devils died. No one's left." And he wiped at his eyes.

I drove back to my base and wrote to Gene.

CHAPTER 23

THE TYPHOON

A Sergeant came in to our tent early one morning to tell us, "Fellers, we got word a big storm is headed our way. So nail everything down and be sure the tent is secure. Good luck." And with that, he turned around and went back out.

Around noon, I could see the sky was full of dark clouds, which looked menacing. After a while the wind increased and the trees were bending slightly. Slowly, slowly, rain began to fall and the wind got stronger.

I left the "office" and stood near a tall tree, watching the passing storm in front of me. The winds got so strong that I grabbed the tree so I wouldn't lose my balance. It was only the middle of the day, but the heavy clouds cut off the sun and it seemed like it was dusk. Then it got darker. The wind began to howl. It seemed alive. I clutched that tree tightly, hung on to it. The wind was cutting, the noise was high-pitched, frightening. It seemed to go on for a long, long time.

Finally, it slowed down and stopped completely. My hands were deeply creased where I had clutched that tree. Lord knows what would have happened to me without it.

I wandered back towards my work tent — but it was *gone*. No other tent was left up, either! All of them had been blown away, along with anything that wasn't nailed down. The Mess Hall, a wooden structure, had its roof missing. Jeeps were rolled over on their sides. What a mess!

Later, we were informed that we had experienced a 140-mile-an-hour typhoon. This never happened in the Bronx.

CHAPTER 24

ME, A MILITARY POLICEMAN

On a troop carrier that was taking the Fifth Bomber Command to another island, a sergeant picked me out of a group of soldiers to be an MP (Military Police). A badge with "MP" on it was wrapped around my arm and I was assigned to guard equipment in the Hold, the very lowest level of the ship. So with my MP badge tied to my upper arm and carrying a carbine, I strolled into a large room piled up with all kinds of boxes, barrels, rolls of cotton and rubber, and other items.

At one point, as I paused and looked around the room, I noticed some movement on a beam at the upper level of a shelf. To my utter horror and disbelief, a huge rat was crouched just fifteen feet away, staring at me. I was scared, really frightened. Never before had I dealt even with mice, and here was a rat the size of a small cat, glaring at me. I could not shoot it, because that would punch a hole in the bottom of the ship and lots of water would pour in.

This ugly creature and I kept staring at each other for about twenty minutes. Finally, the Sergeant arrived along with two other troopers and released me. Was I glad to leave! It was really a horrible episode to remember.

CHARTER 25

THE GAS-SHORTAGE TRIP

We were flying from Clark Field, outside of Mania, to Okinawa. I was in an 8-24 bomber with a full crew of ten men. I had my headset on, so I could hear the talk between the Captain and the various airmen. I was the radio-gunner but there was only radio silence (planes fly with no communication so the enemy can't track them), so I just looked out the side window, resting my arms on the twin 50-caliber machine guns.

Nemo, our navigator, was in a jovial mood. "Yeah," he said, "Cap got us headed jess right." He was a Southerner and spoke with a noticeable accent.

After a couple of hours of small interchanges between them, the Captain asked Nemo, "How near are we to Okinawa?"

Nemo fumbled a bit, harumphed, and answered, "Cap, ahm a leetle fucked up. Got some mix-ups on mah chart."

"Jesus, Nemo," the Captain said, "we've only got a half hour of gas left. Straighten out your charts. Shee-it!"

I glanced at my watch. It was late afternoon. We'd already been aloft a good three hours.

Another fifteen minutes passed.

"Nemo, it's Cap. How we doin?"

"Not so good, Cap. There's some problem here. Can't get it strayette."

"Shit, Nemo — we've got fifteen minutes of gas left!"

I looked down at the Pacific Ocean. Lovely sight. Tiny waves, very peaceful. I realized that if the plane had to land, we *did* have survival rafts. But it was also the case that I couldn't swim. So I began to picture a crash landing in the sea, which we had been lectured about, complete with slides and how to save your life when a plane had to ditch.

"Christ, Nemo, " the Captain shouted, "any luck?"

"No, ahm sorry, Cap."

My watch told me we had about five more minutes left of flying time with the fuel situation. I was really getting edgy, picturing a crash landing, noise, maybe a fire, chaos, water rushing into our cabin. My breath was short.

The nose gunner, Rusty, called in. "Cap, over at the horizon, I see some dot. Might be land." Quiet, no voices. The plane veered slightly, heading toward the far-off dot. It grew bigger. Yes, it turned out to be an island. The plane flew lower and we landed on a piece of land. Later. we learned it was Moratai, an island at the very far end of Indonesia. Lucky us, we still had five minutes of fuel left.

That was "I almost died" Number 1.

CHAPTER 26

STEALING FOOD

Food was a bit of a problem in New Guinea, because it was delivered on a piecemeal basis. Sometimes the food truck would be shelled and destroyed. Or the boat with food would deviate from its course. And who knew if the plane would arrive with all the canned goods we mostly ate? So mealtime was often frustrating.

I had an oddball experience with procuring food.

One night, a guy from Philadelphia named Green who I was friendly with came to my tent and asked me to join him outside. "Evers," he said, "you and I can go down to the Mess Hall where I work all day, and sneak in to get a few cans of fruits and whatever else looks good. Maybe we'll find some chicken soup we can heat up." I stared at him. Why pick me? But I knew it would be cowardly to refuse.

So at night, Green and I walked to the darkened Mess Hall — a square wooden building surrounded by a large wire wrapped around a lot of big bags, sizable cans, and cardboard boxes. We lit matches to locate what we wanted to steal. Then Green took a metal tool and clipped off some wire, reached in, grabbed two large cans, and handed one to me. Then we strolled back to our different tents.

The little bulb in the center of my tent was on, the radio was rattling off the news, and my three tentmates were each doing something or other. "Fellas," I announced, "look what I got." They glanced up and saw my large can of chicken soup.

"Wow," shouted John Morlino, "let's get a fire going. It looks great!"

So Vic, Bill, John, and I lit a fire, heated the can up, opened it and, using our metal cups, enjoyed delicious soup.

Looking back, I now realize that I could have gotten a year in the brig if I had been caught. Not so smart for a boy from the Bronx.

CHAPTER 27

SGT. UDELOWITZ

On a beautiful Sunday morning, on one of my days off, my Bronx pal Bernie Schusky came by my tent. "Hey Lee," he urged, "come with me to have your picture taken."

"What are you talking about?" I asked.

"Sgt. Udelowitz is an aerial photographer. He took his camera out of the bomber he flies and told me to bring a friend and he'd shoot some photographs we could send back home."

"Yeah," I said, "let's go."

So we tramped over to a flat area where Udelowitz was tinkering with some complicated-looking machinery. He glanced up and extended his hand, palm up. I slapped it with mine, we smiled at each other, and he resumed his puttering.

Into the area strode a very tall Sergeant to have his picture taken. His name was Mark Wald, from Santa Ana, California. We conversed about a lot of things — our work, our backgrounds, different experiences we'd had — and we felt quite comfortable with each other, as if we'd known each other for a long time.

Udelowitz asked each of us to sit on a small stool, face him, and smile. He clicked his camera, and then went over to a bucket of liquid and stuck film into it. After a while, he handed me a photograph of myself. It was bee-you-ti-full! I blinked at how handsome I looked, like a movie star. "Thanks, Udelowitz," I told him.

So we sat on the grass, relaxed, talking some more. Udelowitz had a wife and a child and lived in Baltimore.

Wald told us about working on the Santa Ana Mayor's Board of Directors, and working privately as a lawyer. He was married and had a lot of family and friends around him. He looked at me and said, "Lee, you ought to come out to Santa Ana after this fucking war ends and I'll see to it you get a well-paying job. I'll have you meet my family and my friends and find you a place to live. I'll make sure you really enjoy being there."

Of course, I was flattered. He hardly knew me, and yet he had offered me such a wonderful opportunity to start my life off with such success. "Thanks, Mark, you're really so considerate. I'll think about it," I said.

Of course, I could never do that. My wife was tied closely to her mother and her relatives, and I could never leave my Grandma, Dad, or Aunt Bella.

Nevertheless, Brad's offer has stuck in my mind all these years.

CHAPTER 28

THE RADIO BROADCASTER

All the tents had radios. Every night about 6 p.m., when we weren't in motion, a tallish trooper named Levitt read the news to us from US sources (mainly from the "Stars and Stripes" Army newspaper) over the radio.

One morning, on my way to breakfast, Levitt walked alongside me. "Lee, I have to cover General MacArthur for a local news story tomorrow. Could you come over to the Communication Tent and read the six o'clock news?" I looked at him. How the hell did he even know me?

"Sure," I answered. Why not? I thought it would be fun. So the next night, I sat down in front of the transmitter, took the little microphone in my hand, and read off from the sheet I was given.

When I got back to my tent, my three buddies were holding their noses with one hand and putting their thumbs down with the other.

"What did I do wrong?" I asked.

Vic answered, "Lee, you read the news so slow and you pronounced every word too carefully. You stunk."

The next day, Levitt ran over to me and told me that he appreciated my filling in for him. "I'll tell you what happened with MacArthur. All the news guys were filming him and asking him questions as he stepped into a small vessel. It went across the bay to an island our Marines captured a week ago. All of us followed in a different boat. When MacArthur stepped ashore, all kinds of junk was strewn around: cannons, broken tanks, rifles, uniforms, wire — whatever was left over after the battle. Of course, all was quiet. MacArthur gave a short speech and we were handed the Official News Report. Boy, was I surprised. The report claimed that the General entered the combat area when the Japanese soldiers were still shooting at our troops. What colossal nerve he had, lying to the American people like that."

I was very angry about this. *What a fraud*, I thought. *He is nothing but a liar!*"

CHAPTER 29

THE PIECE OF SHRAPNEL

There were many days when the Japanese planes would fly by during the day and spray us with machine-gun bullets. We would all dive onto the ground behind any bushes or trees nearby. At night, occasional Japanese bombers would drop bombs wherever they spotted fires or lights. So we were ordered to build foxholes adjoining our cots. When the bombers came (you could hear the irregular sounds from their motors), we would climb out of our cots and clamber into the foxholes. These were about three feet deep, and if you lay down inside them any bomb shrapnel nearby would fly over you harmlessly. Meanwhile, our anti-aircraft guns tried to hit these invisible planes.

After many nights of these bombings, one night I was so utterly tired that I decided not to go into the foxhole. But the anti-aircraft guns noise and the bomb explosions got me up. I sat on my cot with my elbows on my knees and my hands on the sides of my face. Suddenly, no more than a foot from my head, a red-hot, burning piece of anti-aircraft shrapnel landed between my feet. Wow, did I jump up and get into that foxhole!

Later, I realized that if that chunk of burning metal had landed just a foot closer, it would have hit my head and killed me.

"I almost died" No. 2.

CHAPTER 30

MY PUBLIC-SPEAKING CLASS

On another occasion, I met a trooper named Doucette. He was from Detroit and taught English at Wayne State University, including public speaking. Doucette told me that he had set up a night class to teach anyone who was interested in learning public speaking.

I hurried to the class after dinner. About a dozen guys were sitting on stools. Doucette asked each one of us to tell a five-minute tale that might be interesting to a public gathering.

When my turn came, I told about my work in the Glenram Wine and Liquor Company, which was owned by four former rum-running gangsters who still carried guns and applauded all crooked acts and deeds. My pal Moe (another employee), Lou Zeller (also an employee and a friend) and I set up a scheme to print returns of liquor that would deduct commissions to salesmen. However, the actual amount did not get into the deduction column, and the cheating salesmen kept half the money from the return commissions and split the other half with Moe and me. (This is the fraud I mentioned earlier in Chapter 2.) So Moe and I embarked on a wild time in Manhattan, taking our girlfriends to expensive restaurants, stage plays, and department stores to buy whatever pleased them.

But once the accountant figured out our activities, the four bosses called me into their office and accused me. I admitted my guilt. Eddie Zucker, the main man, shook his head and told me, "Lee, you are one smart son-of-a-bitch." He then smiled, tapped me on my shoulder, and pointed me to the door. I kept my job. Nothing happened.

At the end of my story, everyone clapped their hands, and Doucette came over to me and said,

"Evers, you should be a stand-up comic."

CHAPTER 31

THE ALL-BLACK OUTFIT

What I saw concerning Black soldiers was that almost all were given unimportant work to do, and they rarely saw any front-line action. They were given only support work, never any military duties. It was a shameful episode in US history, I believe.

Anyway, after one of my hospital stays for malaria, my outfit had moved on and I was left behind and ordered to move in with an Engineering section for one week. It was a Black outfit, with a white lieutenant in charge. It consisted of sixty-four Black soldiers! I was surprised.

So they gave me a cot, and showed me the shower, the Mess Hall, and where to borrow books. They were very friendly. I kept imagining how a Black person felt when surrounded by all white people. My Bronx background made me familiar with their mostly big-city cultures back in the US. We ate together, put up poles for electricity together, straightened roads, and played cards without difficulty.

The one thing I still recall clearly was when Harris, a Cincinnati soldier, asked me to go with three others for a jeep ride to a Manila-area whore house. I did not want to seem unfriendly, so I told Harris I'd go along but didn't want to fuck a whore. He was all right with that, and after mess the four of us drove downtown to a building with a red flag hanging from it. General MacArthur had ordered these hostels to be set up to service the men while preventing the spread of disease.

We entered a large room with chairs all around. A neatly dressed woman spoke to my companions, and they went off into a hallway and waved to me to join them. Harris pulled a curtain behind me, took of his clothes, and walked into the woman's room. The other two men walked into other rooms where women were waiting. Meanwhile, I waited in the downstairs room with a cup of coffee.

On the ride back, each guy gave a description of his experiences. I sat there quietly, a bit stunned to have been part of this escapade. Thinking back, I realize how the men were, how easily I fit in and did pretty much everything they did. I noticed no differences between these Black soldiers and their white-soldier counterparts. So racial differences are a joke. The only difference I noticed was that some people were sunburned and some people had black skin.

After the war, the head Sergeant, Sgt. Eustace, whom I often chatted with, came to the Bronx to visit my tentmate Vic Klodin. Vic invited me to drop by. The Sarge and I warmly shook hands, and he made me feel the uniqueness of those days gone by.

CHAPTER 32

THE MOVIE AND THE JAPANESE ATTACK

My Colonel ordered me to go to Indonesia, drop off supplies, and come back. So off I flew for a few hundred miles, deposited the plane full of materials, signed various forms, and was driven back to a tent closer to where the plane landed. As I was eating supper, I heard that an infantry group was going to see a movie on the nearby hill, so I wandered up the hill. It was dark by this time, and I saw guys stretching a white sheet between some trees to make a movie screen. Then three men carried a movie camera to a small platform and — presto fandango! — a movie began. I was enthralled. I had not seen a film in over a year!

About halfway through, we heard the uneven motor sounds of the Japanese planes. Suddenly, bombs were being dropped nearby. What an unbelievably loud uproar ensued! On top of this deafening noise, we heard machine guns being sprayed at us. Boy, did we all scramble down the hill! We threw ourselves down, with our hands over our unhelmetted heads.

Finally, it was over. Quiet. So we clambered back to see the movie end. It was all an indescribable experience, and it taught me that I could survive almost anything.

CHAPTER 33

GENERAL JOE STILLWELL

In the jungle one day, on Moratai I think, I had a very intriguing experience, which I continue to remember with great clarity.

As my jeep was driving the usual road — kind of a cow track through large, overhanging trees on both sides — I heard the sound of a large motor approaching. (To pass on these tight roads, one vehicle had to pull over into the dense underbrush to allow the other to get by.) A large truck filled with armed men came abreast of me. I pulled over, the truck drove past, and a jeep came after it. It stopped — and I was staring at General Joe Stillwell, Commander in Chief of our Asian forces. He probably had been meeting with General MacArthur to coordinate their command operations.

I had never met such a highly placed military person in my life. He looked so impressive, a real Commander.

CHAPTER 34

CHEMICAL WARFARE

Another unforgettable incident occurred when I was carrying all sorts of secret memos and vital papers to various departments. One day I saw John Morlino, my tentmate, in an office with his Colonel-boss sitting nearby. It was the Chemical Division. I stopped to say hello and ask what was going on.

The Colonel noticed me and waved to me to come to his section. "You're Lee, aren't you, from the Engineers?"

"Yes, sir," I responded.

"Did John ever explain what we do in this area?"

"No, never, sir."

"Well, let me tell you a bit about our purpose. We know from our spy agencies that the Japanese military is capable of using chemical weapons and even poison gas. Even though it's been barred internationally, they have the capacity to utilize these if they deem it necessary. Perhaps if they were losing the war, they might think it's necessary to attack us with these weapons. So we keep poison gas on hand, should that happen. We also have a wide array of other illegal materials available to retaliate, should they use them against us. The nature of these materials is secret — but you, as a soldier, should be secure in knowing that our armed forces can respond to virtually any unexpected or uncalled for chemical attack."

I thanked the Colonel profusely, letting him know how relieved I was to learn about our response-ability.

Experiences like this one made me aware of how our government operates. The public is mostly unaware of what utterly horrible materials we have secretly stored away, should someone unleash their dangerous but illegal weapons on us. It's very scary.

CHAPTER 35

NO PROMOTION

My Colonel, Colonel Imb, was a pleasant man who had a lot of officers coming into our work area. He chased whatever women were available — nurses, Red Cross workers, reporters, and so forth — and let me run the Air Engineers Office by signing a bunch of blank slips, which I had to decide how to distribute and to whom.

One day, there was a notice on the Bulletin Board stating that Promotion Day was due. I expected the Colonel to promote me to Corporal; it was called for. Instead, he elevated six others.

I was hurt. "Colonel," I asked him, "why didn't you promote me? I have it coming."

"Look, Evers, you never come by my tent to bring up bottled water or fix the plywood floor or put new bulbs in when mine die. So I gave those men who help me an upgrade."

I got it. It was not my work that counted, but personal favors to the Colonel. I decided never to talk to the Colonel about anything but the job. He resented it, but never mentioned it to me.

Eventually, he was promoted to General White's staff, and a sharp West Point Captain took over. He berated me, threatened me, and fired me. I was given other work.

Thanks, Colonel.

CHAPTER 36

LOVELY FAILE

In a small Philippine town called Tacloban, I was on guard duty from 1 a.m. to 5 a.m. Among our huge piles of materials was a tall stack of plywood sheets, each one 4 x 8 feet. A young Pilipino approached me and pointed to the plywood. He said, in imperfect English, "My house has no floor. My wife, daughter, and mother walk on earth and grass all day. We're very poor. Those Japanese took all that we owned. Can I take one of those sheets of plywood to use in our small house?"

"Sure," I told him. *Why not*, I thought, *America is rich. We can afford one piece of wood for this man.* He clambered up, pulled down one sheet, held it over his head, and walked into the darkness.

The next night, as I patrolled the area, he showed up again. "Would you come to our house for a cup of coffee, whenever you can?" he asked.

"Where's your home?" I asked. He pointed it out. "I'll be at your house tonight, say 6 o'clock." My Chicago pal, Ron Thompson, gave me a pass, and that evening I wandered over. The house was a thinly made wooden structure. I walked into their one large room with a closed-door section.

"My name is Juan," the man I'd given the plywood to announced, and he pointed to his wife Angelina, then to his mother, Juliette, and his very pretty sixteen-year-old daughter. "Her name is Faile," he told me.

I smiled at all of them, accepted the coffee his wife handed me and the odd-tasting cake or whatever it was, and his mother beamed at me and spoke in Spanish to Juan. He turned to me and said, "My mother wants you to be the first man that Faile will make love to. So through that door, you'll find a bed." I assumed it was their thank-you for the plywood.

The Grandma gave Faile instructions, and the girl opened the door for me. "Gee," I thought, "what a treat. A virgin. Holy smokes, this is really something special." In the dimly lit room, Faile began to disrobe.

But then there was a lot of loud talk outside the room. We stopped to see what was up. Would you believe it, three relatives had stopped by for a visit, just that evening! So Faile put her clothes back on and left the room. When I came out, Juan ushered me to the front door and told me it was too bad.

The next morning, I was on a truck, going to a plane and flying to a new island.

Such a strange experience! Just for kicks, Juan had handed me a photograph of his pretty daughter, Faile. I was happy to have it, and I thanked him. I showed the photo to the other guys on the truck. One guy from Iowa asked me to lend it to him to mail to his family so they'd know what Pilipinos looked like. He promised me he'd return it, but he never did, and we went our separate ways.

I sure would have enjoyed looking at her photo now and then.

CHAPTER 37

INVITATIONS TO MOVE

Some odd things happened to me in the war. For whatever reason, three soldiers at different times asked me to move from New York City to their towns and live with them. They offered to get me jobs, introduce me to their friends and relatives, and give me a really good life. I wish I knew why they decided I was so special to them.

One of them was Jack Williams, who worked in transmissions and lived in McGill, Nevada, about fifty miles south of Las Vegas. He had some involvement in mining. As we were walking towards the Mess Hall one day, he invited me to come and live in his town. "Jack," I told him, "I'm married and couldn't possibly join you. But your offer is beautiful. Thanks."

Then there was Brownie. His actual name was Brown, and I never knew his first name. He lived in a small town way up in Northern California, not far from the Oregon border. We spent three weeks together in Yokohama, waiting for transportation back to the U.S. because the war had ended. At some point, after two weeks of hanging around the huge aircraft base waiting for our names to be called to be assigned to a plane or naval vessel, Brownie told me he believed I would fit into his town perfectly. He said his family and friends would surround me and offer me whatever I sought. "Why not move, Evers?" he asked. Again, I explained what I had told Jack Williams. Brownie shook his head and told me, "Lee, you're missing a great chance to have a really great way to live."

The other person who wanted me to move was Mark Wald from Santa Ana, California, mentioned in Chapter 27.

Three times I declined, offered warm thanks, and planned to stay in New York. But to this day, as I near 101 years of age, I look back and wonder why these three soldiers thought I should live near them.

CHAPTER 38

THE YWCA IN MANILA

During a three-day pass, four of us went to nearby Manila and hired a one-man jitney cart to drive us around. My three pals went to the whorehouse. This kind of thing was sanctioned by General MacArthur, and set up so the women would be medically examined weekly to avoid passing illnesses around in the troops.

I walked around town and found a sign, "YWCA." I went in, and the director, Mrs. Gomez, a Puerto Rican woman from the Bronx, no less, told me to stay over and attend their activities. There were gymnastics, ballet, singing, dancing, and meals in the dining area. Once I ate with the Manila Chief of Police. I stayed for three days and returned twice more.

The strange thing was, I had not realized that the YWCA (the Young Women's Christian Association) was not the same as the YMCA (the Young Men's Christian Association)! So by calmly entering this very attractive building, I had expected that a lot of men would be exercising or drinking coffee in the dining area. But Mrs. Gomez, realizing I had made an error, assured me that it was fine; I could sleep over.

Imagine being the only man among 100 women! It was a memorable event in my life. I adored Mrs. Gomez.

CHAPTER 39

THREE-DAY CELEBRATION

One morning, a young Pilipino entered our tent and invited us to a three-day celebration. Of the four of us (John, Bill, Vic and me), I was the only one who accepted.

The young Pilipino and I tramped through the jungle and came to a river. Since I couldn't swim, I climbed on the young man's back and he crossed the river standing up. Considering his small size, he was really a strong person!

We arrived at a small village where everyone was dressed in tuxedos and flowing gowns in bright colors. A large band played and everyone danced. Wine flowed, and there was food all over. It went on for three days. I slept on and off among a bunch of young women. The mayor praised me for being the only US soldier to celebrate with them.

Wherever I went — to the dance floor, or the numerous tables stacked with delicious-looking food, or to the sleeping area — everyone was so warm and friendly. The celebration was for being freed from the Japanese invaders. So I was very special to the villagers.

CHAPTER 40

NATIVE VILLAGES

I had a day off and was sitting on my cot reading a book that the "library on wheels" had offered me, when my buddies Jorgensen and Sundstrom, two big Swedes, stuck their heads in and asked me if I'd join them on a hike along the river bank going up the large mountain nearby. "No thanks, fellers. I'm happy reading," I said.

"Come on," Jorgensen said, "you'll like the adventure." Sundstrom smiled, put his hands in his pockets, and nodded.

"Okay, okay," I told them and put the book aside. I got my carbine, a vacuum bottle of water, and some snacks, and we strolled along the river road, gradually moving up a slight rise. Suddenly we came upon a small village where the natives had put up odd-shaped homes of tree leaves bound together at the ceilings, and tree sections stuck deep in the earth that protected them from the rain. Oddly, the natives were nude.

One Aussie was the headman, since New Guinea was owned by Australia. He pointed out interesting things. For example: The natives drew low tree branches together and made a shelter for sleeping. All the children were raised by the whole village. The different villages specialized in different products, which they shared with each other. But I was totally arrested by a native who clambered up a tree just like a squirrel, and came down with a large pineapple. One young man with a bow and arrow was flexing the bow. I put my pack of Lucky Strike cigarettes in a tree limb twenty feet away. He casually pulled out an arrow, fitted it in the bow and zing! — it hit the center of the little circle on the cigarette box!

We walked another half mile and came to another village. This one was similar to the first, but full of pigs. Obviously, they traded pigs for food and other necessities. We were treated quite nicely and we handed out some things like peanuts, candy, and cigarettes, which they loved.

In a third village, as we entered through the tall wooden gates, I noticed human skulls on top of some of the poles. In this village, the decorated witch doctor explained to the Aussie official, they were warriors and hunted wild animals. Whenever there was a confrontation over land or women, they would fight other villages. *Scary,* I thought.

In the last village we saw that day, it was quiet and peaceful, with lots of little children running around. The Aussie explained that here, every child belonged to every villager, so the entire community was one huge family.

Hmm, I thought, *why don't we try that in America?*

CHAPTER 41

PARACHUTISTS

At one point, we learned that the Japanese had attacked a nearby anti-aircraft position. One of the soldiers from the group that had been attacked clambered up the hill where we were camped. He was frightened and told us of the surprise attack.

Late that afternoon, we heard the broken, rough noises that emanated from Japanese planes. Looking up, I counted fifteen planes and could plainly see their red circles on the sides. Suddenly, large white bundles came spilling out of the airplanes. They expanded in size and turned out to be parachutes with soldiers holding their rifles, landing all around our small hillock. I learned afterwards that these were the best soldiers of the Japanese army, called the "Imperial Marines."

Top Sgt. Luz had us all line up and he issued orders: four men to a foxhole twenty yards apart all around our hillside. We had about 600 men in our command post, and all of us got busy. From a truck loaded with shovels, we each grabbed one and found a spot to dig. I was digging along with three other guys I didn't know. We dug with shovels, spades, and whatever else could move earth. As it began to get dark, four of us were standing in the foxhole, facing the flatland down below, guns in our arms. We were located atop a small hillock rising gently from the field. It was dark, and there was no talking.

The patrol came by. Sgt. Luzo asked, "You guys okay? Need smokes? Coffee?" We were duly supplied, and the patrol left. It was tense. We could hear the Japanese calling to each other below. They could have easily climbed up the small incline, about twenty feet high, to where we were.

As we stood there, one man said, "I feel sick, I better get over to the medical tent." He began to clamber out of the foxhole.

"I'll help him," another man called.

They left, and then there was only me and another GI in the foxhole. About an hour passed and this soldier said to me, "I better go see what's holding up those two guys." He climbed out, and I was alone.

The time passed achingly slowly. I had my carbine in front of me, aimed into the air. I pictured Japanese soldiers suddenly appearing before me. I imagined firing my rifle and them returning fire. I pictured them tossing grenades into my foxhole. It was scary. I sweated, I scratched myself, I cursed the three men who had left me alone. Where was that darned patrol? Nothing moved. Only the voices below, talking in a strange language. Believe me, I was frightened. I trembled when the voices got closer and closer.

Eventually, they faded. The night passed slowly, slowly. Nothing happened.

Dawn broke, the patrol came by. I got coffee. Sgt. Luzo said, "Evers, you're relieved. Other soldiers will occupy the foxhole." I climbed out, feeling very relieved.

Looking back, I never was so frightened for so long ever in my life.

"I almost died" No. 3.

CHAPTER 42

THE ANTI-AIR CRAFTERS

During this period when we were surrounded by Japan's best fighters, The Imperial Marines, we had to creep or crawl our way to get food, to sleep, or do the various duties to which we were assigned as well as to urinate or defecate. It was a difficult period. Try living all day by crawling on the ground.

But the Japanese soldiers had tied themselves to tree tops and constantly fired at moving targets. We survived, but it was a hellish time. We grouped around our small hilltop and when we heard firing — mostly from some individual Japanese tied to a treetop — a bunch of us would aim our rifles at that target and release a barrage of bullets, hoping we'd kill the son-of-a-bitch.

After about ten days of isolation, to our delight a dozen anti-aircraft soldiers clambered up our hill. These guys were infantry-trained and immediately, after a quick meal, held hands while slowly descending the small hill. At the bottom, they carefully, step by step, moved through the bushes, grass, and trees towards the Japanese-held area. Suddenly I heard the *brrp* of machine-gun fire and rapid rifle shots as the men discovered the enemy. As they disappeared from sight, I continued to hear discordant shots.

A few hours later, the troopers crawled back up the hill, all sweaty and in torn, dirty uniforms. "Well," a sergeant said to a large group of our guys, "we killed all the bastards!" We all yelled and screamed. Our nightmare was over.

CHAPTER 43

NO JAPANESE PRISONERS

One of the infantry men who had just been in the battle came to our tent for some rest and fell asleep on the floor. The next morning, before we all headed to the Mess Tent, he told us a strange tale. "You guys don't know it, but we never take Japanese prisoners."

"Why not?" I asked him.

"My buddies doing patrols surrounded about five Japanese who held their hands up. When they got close, one of the Japanese soldiers reached down, grabbed a grenade off his belt and threw it at us. One of the group died, one was hurt. On another patrol, we found a group of Japanese, who surrendered. My buddy told me they indicated to them to take their clothes off. Naked, they came towards our men. This time one of them reached behind and took out a grenade he had stuck up his ass and threw it at our guys. So they never took prisoners again."

Neither did we. We're not stupid, you know.

CHAPTER 44

UNDER SIEGE

During the nine days after the Japanese Imperial Marines had parachuted into our area and captured a small airport and killed some anti-aircraft soldiers, we were continuously under attack. A number of their camouflaged men had climbed into the trees, and took shots at whatever moved on our hillock. We were surrounded.

General White, commander of our 5th Bomber Command, had sent orders for us to "hold the hill." Since we weren't infantry, ground fighting was a new experience. We were trained for bombers. Our days consisted of foxhole duties, trips to the mess tent, to the latrines and to our own tents for sleep. Whenever we were near the edge of the hill, we had to crawl in order to avoid the snipers in the trees. One day, a team of twenty-four veteran foot-soldiers showed up. One of them moved into my tent for a night. Next morning, he stood at the end of my foxhole.

"Get down, Mac," I told him, "you'll be shot."

"Fuck 'em," he said. Sure enough, a bullet plunked into a nearby tree. Mac didn't budge. He strode around, ignoring the danger. Go figure.

In my case, one day at lunch time, I climbed out of my foxhole and crawled away from the danger area, then rose and walked to the Mess Hall, bent over to avoid being a target. There, I got some food on my metal mess pan and went over to a corner, where I squatted down to eat my lunch. The Mess Hall was a four-posted squarish building with a tarpaulin for a roof. It was enclosed by Hessian cloth, a tan-colored fuzzy kind of fabric that resisted the intense heat and perhaps discouraged bugs and snakes from entering.

Another G.I., small-sized and blond-haired, whom I recognized but didn't know very well, squatted down opposite me. "How's it going?" he asked.

"Nothing special," I said. I was very tired from about a week of this new routine. As I munched my food, my eyes rested on the Hessian cloth. Suddenly, like magic, a spot on the cloth opened and closed. The G.I. opposite me, who was in a crouching position like mine, shrieked, "I'm shot! I've been shot!" I looked at him. His knee, which was at my eye-level, was bleeding profusely. If that bullet had been nine inches closer, it would have hit my head. Lucky me.

"I almost died" No. 4.

CHAPTER 45

ANZAKS

I was sent out on various missions by Colonel Imb, often when the marines were fighting for a foothold on some small island. Occasionally I'd meet soldiers from Australia and New Zealand. They were extraordinarily brave, venturing into battle zones (unlike our more careful soldiers). We called them ANZAKS, for <u>A</u>ustralians <u>N</u>ew <u>Z</u>ealand <u>acks</u>.

When I asked these soldiers about their supplies, such as planes, tanks, trucks, or guns, one of them pointed to a large heap of abandoned materials that the US troops had discarded. "We pick through your pile of junk and fix 'em up," he told me. "Yes, we repair your planes and tanks, because your men always want new materials and we're not as choosy."

I admired them intensely. They didn't have the productive facilities that Americans had — we just threw things away and got new ones — but they were so happy to be able to scavenge through our junk and fix their planes with our stuff.

Ever since my encounter with these unusually stalwart fighters, whenever I meet or talk to a person who is connected with either country, I make it a point to tell them how heroic their soldiers were. "Tell your dads and uncles we really appreciated how hard they fought in the war." Doing this makes me feel good.

CHAPTER 46

YELLOW JAUNDICE

Some months later, on Mindoro Island in the Philippines, I was unable to wake up one morning. I felt terrible: my head hurt, my mouth tasted awful, I was feverish and could not move.

A Sergeant came in to find out why I hadn't shown up for work.

"I don't feel good," I croaked.

"Shit," he said, "go to the medical tent."

So, very, very slowly, I pulled on my shorts and shoes and blundered in a smokey yellowish haze from one tree to another until I got to the medical tent. A medic ran over, lowered me to the ground, put a thermometer in my mouth, read it — and in what seemed like a moment, I was transported by ambulance to a field hospital.

I was unconscious for five days.

When I awoke, a nurse was rubbing my back and talking to another nurse at the next bed. "Oh, you're up," she exclaimed, turning to face me. "High time. You've been asleep for five days. You've had Yellow Jaundice."

Another nurse chimed in and told me the same story I had heard during an earlier time about having malaria — that if I had been left untreated for a few more hours, I would have perished from my temperature of 106. "You're a really lucky soldier," she said. "Once we established the severe nature of your illness, three nurses were assigned to massage your entire body with alcohol for eight-hour shifts each. It was a sweat, but we kept your fever down, and now you're safe."

The nurse told me she was from Sheboygan, Wisconsin. I will never forget her: small, ordinary-looking, and caring.

"I almost died" No. 5.

CHAPTER 47

THE GOLD STORY

In the next bed at this hospital was a red-headed guy. We never spoke until my last afternoon there, when I had recovered from the liver ailment and went for chow. He was on the chow line too. "Hey," he exclaimed, turning to me and offering his hand, "I'm Wilson. We have beds next to each other." So we chatted.

Wilson lived in Northern California, where he had a mom, dad, and sister. He told me quite a story. He was in the Tank gunnery and his unit was in a battle. He got injured, a Purple Hearter. After recovering, he and his sidekick, Pete, decided they needed a break. So they loaded up the provisions, stole a jeep, and headed into the jungle. Arriving in a small village, they gave out candy, cigarettes, and canned food to the locals, and they were warmly welcomed. Pete used to be a gold miner from Idaho, so when he spotted a large cave he went over to examine it. "Hey, Wilson," yelled Pete, "come over here!" and Wilson did.

Pete pointed to a wall inside the huge cave and told Wilson that it was almost pure gold. He also said there were other veins of gold all over the cave! Pete drew an exact map of where they were by following the path they had taken from their base, including every marker they could remember and whatever information they could glean from the Witch Doctor. (Each village had a Witch Doctor, and the chief would listen to his advice because he was supposed to be in touch with God.) Then, they emptied their bags full of provisions, gave them to the chief as a thank-you, and directed him to place one native in front of the cave daily to guard it, and not to let anyone in until they came back.

Wilson and Pete drove back to base, were punished with KP duties for a week for not notifying the commanding officer that they were going to be off base, and were ordered back to attack Japanese positions. Pete was killed — but Wilson had the map. He told me he had mailed it to his sister in California and hoped to arrange a trip with trusted men to dig out the gold when he got back home.

What a tale! I kept picturing myself as part of their group and earning a suitcase full of gold.

CHAPTER 48

THE THREE-PLANE MISSION

When we invaded Leyte, New Guinea, my Colonel told me, "Evers, we've loaded up a plane with our vital equipment. Be aboard at Nadzab airport at 4 a.m. tomorrow. Get the stuff to our new campsite."

So, in the dark, I was jeeped to the plane. Actually, it was a three-plane trip, all B-25s (medium- sized bombers). My ship was full of shovels, bags of cement, pipes, mechanical doodads of all kinds . . . whatever my Air Engineer command needed to run our 600-man camp.

We took off as dawn arrived. It was a pleasant ride from the tip of New Guinea to the island that our forces had invaded two days earlier. As we neared the island, we saw occasional ack-ack fire (the sound of the anti-aircraft guns) aimed at fighter planes aiding the bomber planes involved in the invasion. Boy, it was scary! One piece of flak could knock our ship down. To my relief, we landed safely, and I hopped down on secure ground. Other men, whom I didn't know, were actual crew members of these planes.

Just as we got down, a motorcycle drove up and a red-headed, sweaty Sergeant from the Military Police got off and asked for the top officer — a Major. The two of them spoke, and then the Major turned to us and said, "Men, the Japanese fleet is coming up the Sanbao Straights. If they get through, they could cut off our forces. We've been ordered to load up with 500 pounders and attack their fleet." Three jeeps were pulling in all around our planes, which had been shunted off to the side of the newly built, rather beat-up field. The jeeps were pulling little trailers each holding 2,500-pound bombs, which were then attached to the bottom of these B-25s.

While all this was going on, all the equipment in my plane had been unloaded onto the ground and was piled up in a kind of pyramid shape. "Okay, men," the Colonel called out, "back on the ships. We're taking off."

"Just a minute," shouted the Red-headed sergeant, "someone's gotta watch this big pile. I got other duties to attend to." The Colonel glanced around, spotted me as the outsider and said, "Soldier, stay here and watch the equipment." It was my section's supplies. They all boarded the planes, moved over the abutment to the main field and, in moments, were aloft.

I sat down and watched planes coming and going. Off in the distance, I could see ack-ack bursts and our planes flying around, and hear the usual noises of warfare. Sometime later, one of the planes arrived back and then a second one came as well. The guys got off.

I asked one G.I., "When's my plane coming?"

"That one was hit; it went down." That was a shock. The very plane I would have been on had been downed!

There was no way of knowing what had happened to the men who'd been aboard. As far as I knew, a crippled plane that went down into the ocean rarely had any survivors. Some guys could parachute, and some could remain afloat if they could get out; but for the most part, I knew they would have all drowned. So for whatever reason, I was spared.

"I almost died" No. 6.

CHAPTER 49

THE GAY SOLDIER

In Luzon, my Bronx friend Bernie Schursky asked me if I'd like to take a ride up to a northern town in the Philippines called Bagio, where our 5th Bomber Command friend, Rosen, had a relative. "Sure, Bernie," I told him. So on Friday night, the three of us took a two-and-a-half-hour jeep ride to Bagio. The town was full of soldiers, many of whom had passes, as we did. They were all over town in bars, restaurants, ships, and wherever.

Rosen found his relative, and we all were comfortable together. At about 1 a.m., Rosen's relative left and the rest of us headed toward our jeep. A soldier, seemingly a bit drunk, walked past us and loudly announced, "Anybody want their cock sucked? I'll do it. Anybody, just come on over."

Was I surprised! The three of us smiled at each other and shrugged our shoulders. What could be crazier?

Another startling event took place one day when I walked past a certain tent inhabited by two guys — a fellow called Rose, and the other was Bauer. They often stopped me to talk. We'd discuss things like the radio news, plans for the upcoming ballgame, and the Mess Hall food. They were very pleasant men.

A few times, passing their tent, I had noticed that it was empty, and it was empty now, too. So when a soldier strolled by, I asked him where the heck Bauer and Rose were.

"Those two jerks were fags," he explained. "They were brought up on charges, dismissed, and shipped back to Washington."

Wow! I had never dealt with gay guys in my lifetime, so this was way over my head. In those days, I guess being gay was a crime. What a strange thing for an innocent youngster from the Bronx to run into.

CHAPTER 50

CAPTAIN ECKHART'S FLIGHT

Captain Eckhart was a very likable guy. He smiled a lot, had a big shock of tan-colored hair, and didn't put on an officer act. He'd flown his fifty combat missions and been assigned to our Air Engineer group.

One day he came over to my desk and asked if I'd fly up to Vella Lavella with him. He needed a hand with some project. Since I couldn't refuse anyway, I said, "Sure." We got into a small air ship of some kind, wheeled around to the main airstrip, roared down the strip, and went into the air.

On the short flight, I could see the ocean, beaches, jungles, even some huts the natives put up in their little villages. We began to fly lower to the ground, just a little above the trees. The small airport runway loomed ahead. I was standing behind Captain Eckhart as he touched different knobs and buttons, lowering the aircraft. We touched down. The gravel created a jarring sound, but we landed smoothly.

Unfortunately, at the end of the runway, there were tall trees. As we rapidly approached them, the Captain cursed, hunched his shoulders, and uttered, "Damn, damn, damn!" as we headed towards the trees. I was scared. At the last moment, the Captain threw the plane into a sharp turn, almost in reverse. But we were safe.

"Whew!" the Captain said. Then he added, "You know, Evers," wiping an accumulation of sweat from his brow, "this is the closest I've ever come to dying in all my fifty combat missions."

I wiped off a little sweat too.

"I almost died" No. 7.

CHAPTER 51

THE RUBBER RAFT

"Get up, Ayvers, our day off!" Carmen Winnard yelled at me. (He talked that way because he was from Mississippi.)

I rubbed my eyes and pulled on shorts. "What have you got in mind for us, Carmen?" I asked. He and I had been left behind for a few days to clear up the camp. We had local villagers to do the work. We just told them what to do, and they loaded up the trucks with material that would be shipped by boat to our next camp.

"Ah got a rubber boat . . . the emergency raft from a guy. It's got two paddles. We can row out to the sunken Japanese ship," he said.

Out in the bay, there was a sunken Japanese freighter about 150 yards away. Only the very top of the ship could be seen. A small platform with a pole coming out of its center was visible, but as the waves washed over the vessel you could see the rest of the ship under the waves.

So Carmen and I took along some bread and gum and cigarettes, and carried the rubber dingy down to the beach. We put it into the ocean and jumped into it, and then began paddling towards the ship. The paddles were tiny, about a foot long, and were intended only to get the raft to a nearby place.

It was sunny, with a pleasant wind. We were on the Philippine Island of Mindoro, and as we paddled toward the ship we could see a long finger of land reaching out into the ocean on one side. Otherwise, there was nothing but ocean everywhere. It was quite peaceful.

We reached the ship and pulled our rubber raft onto the platform. I was tired, so I stretched out with my legs in the water and closed my eyes to shield them from the sunshine. "Ayvers, wake up," called Carmen. "Ah storm is coming up."

I looked around. The sky was grey; the air was heavy. It looked like a tropical storm was about to break. This kind of thing happened often and quickly in those areas. We got into our raft, pushed it away from the platform, and began padding towards the beach, but we didn't move too much because the tide was against us. We rowed harder and faster but were being driven away from the beach. *Lord*, I thought, *I can't swim. If we're pulled away from the shore, what will happen to us?* I was all sweated up.

The sky was darker, the wind stronger. We kept drifting further and further from our beach into the ocean. Looming ahead was the extended finger of land. We wouldn't hit it but would pass it by about thirty yards. We kept paddling, but our tiny paddles had little impact on the wave.

Just then, two trucks full of G.I.s pulled in to the end of the jutting land. "Help, help," we yelled, waving our paddles. The soldiers began jumping into the ocean, and in a short time one of them — held by a man behind him who was part of a chain of swimmers — grasped the edge of our raft. Gradually, they all pulled our raft to shore.

Now the storm had begun in earnest. The Major in charge put us in his jeep and drove us the short distance to our own camp. We thanked him and told him his men had saved our lives. He said, "You'd do the same for us."

"I almost died" No. 8.

CHAPTER 52

FDR'S DEATH

I was sitting at my desk, deeply involved with straightening out some clutter, when Turk entered. He was a tall guy, broad, dark-complected, and unshaven. "Listen, Evers," he uttered very slowly, "Roosevelt died."

"No way!" I screamed. I jumped up and moved closer to him. "Turk, you bastard, that's not true!" I shouted.

He looked down at his shoes. "It's true — just heard it on the radio. He's dead."

"Turk," I uttered coldly, "I'll bet you ten fucking dollars that Roosevelt's alive." Turk nodded and slowly turned around and walked away.

I eventually paid up.

CHAPTER 53

GUY VAN

Guy Van was from Quincy, Massachusetts. He looked like a young Franklin D. Roosevelt and had a Boston accent. He stood out in our makeshift touch-football, softball, and volley-ball games. I'd met Guy back at Scott Field, near St. Louis, where we taught Morse Code for use on planes. We ended up together in Lae, New Guinea and remained friends.

One day, after spending four hours in the burning sun loading fifty-pound ammo boxes from an anchored freighter onto our trucks, Guy asked me if I wanted to go swimming in the ocean to wash off the dirt and sweat we'd picked up on our duty. "No, Guy," I told him, "you go. I don't know how to swim. I'll shower at the camp." Soon work ended. He walked over to the back of a truck that had two other G.I.s on it and jumped in. He sat with his feet dangling over the edge, waved at me, and went off.

I trudged back to camp and got into a makeshift shower, which consisted of a hose that emptied into an old paint can we had punched holes into, hung atop a sheet-metal enclosure. After that, I walked to my tent and stretched out on my cot.

"Evers, Evers." I opened my eyes and at the entrance to my tent stood Turk, the big, dark-haired man who had told me about FDR dying. "I just got the news about Guy. He was killed."

"What," I exploded, "whaddaya talking about?" I was on my feet, walking towards Turk. "We just unloaded trucks together at the dock," I said.

"Yeah, I know," said Turk. "Guy was on a truck, sitting on the edge. A Duck" — a four-wheeled land-and-sea vehicle with a prow up front — "turned and knocked Guy's head off!"

I wanted to wail. Guy dead? He was just right here.

Turk backed out of the tent. "See ya," he mumbled and walked off.

I sat down on the cot. How could this terrible thing have happened? It hurt. Guy — Guy Van — with his Boston accent. I wept. No one came along, and I just sat there holding my head and cried.

Looking back so many years later, I realize that if I'd taken Guy up on his offer to take a dip in the ocean, it might just as well have been me who sat on the side of the truck, legs dangling over the edge as it slowly moved along the rough pathway to the main road where that Duck hit Guy's head and tore it off. How many times have I thought of writing a letter to the people with the last name of Van in Quincy, MA, to let them know how highly regarded Guy was, and what a durable and uncomplaining soldier he was. I kept imagining myself going to Quincy and phoning all the Vans until I located his family. Then I would visit them to tell them all I knew about Guy.

I never did it, and I have regretted it for these seventy-five-odd years.

However, in a library one day not long ago, I looked up a phone book that did cover Quincy. I found more than ten people listed there named Van.

Another final note about Guy: He was friendly with a rough-edged New Jersey soldier, Bill Lenich, who I also knew from radio-gunnery school at Scott Field. Bill had typical Polish features: a longish, slightly bent nose, high cheekbones, and a very intelligent pair of grayish eyes. I met him on the chow line a few days after Guy's death.

"You know, Evers," Lenich said, "after this fucking war is over, I'm going to Quincy and look up Guy's family. He told me he has a sister. If it goes okay, maybe she and I will get together."

I sure hope he did. It would make me feel much better about Guy if Bill pulled this off. At least he'd be able to tell Guy's family what a decent man Guy was.

"I almost died" No. 9.

CHAPTER 54

U.S.S. MISSOURI

I was in Okinawa in the China sea, miles from Japan, when I heard that Japan had surrendered. I was so pleased, because otherwise we expected to lose 400,000 soldiers in order to overcome their defenses. I could easily have been one of them.

One day, into our harbor steamed the huge battleship U.S.S. Missouri. From the radio, we learned that this would be where Japan's Prime Minster would sign surrender papers. My tent was on a hill, so I could clearly see the ship. As I watched, a small craft approached the ship Men in immaculate clothes climbed aboard, and the crew smartly saluted them. Of course, these were all dignitaries from Australia, Britain, India, Malaysia, the Philippines, etc. who were participating in the surrender. It was truly thrilling to be a close observer of World War II's end.

CHAPTER 55

THE NEW SMOKER

I was in Okinawa, waiting to go home. I went to the main tent and spoke to a Major there. "Look," I told him, "it's two-and-a-half years that I've been in this war. MacArthur has moved to Tokyo, where all the action will take place to get us G.I.s home. Can you send me to Tokyo?"

"Sure, Soldier," he told me, "I'll write you a flight number right now."

So I flew to Tokyo and was sent to live in a vast airplane hangar in Yokohama. It was lined from one end to the other with sleeping cots for at least 2,000 men. In the center, a very large speaker called out the names of soldiers and told them to go to different piers, airport sections, submarine bases, and whatever locations were involved in sending troops back to the U.S.A.

It took three weeks until my name was called. In the interim, forced to be in the hangar, I smoked my first cigarette. By the end of that period, I was smoking two packs a day! I kept smoking for the next fifty-five years.

CHAPTER 56

BROWNIE

In Yokohama, as we waited for our names to be called, I became friendly with the guy on the neighboring cot. He was a slim, dark-haired fellow whose name was "Brownie" (short for Brown, of course). We ate our meals together in the enclosed mess area, strolled around the huge airplane hangar, smoked constantly, and talked about our previous life experiences.

After I had filled him in about my job, New York University, Cooper Union, my friendships, and my wife, Brownie stopped walking and faced me squarely. "Evers, I think you and your wife should move out to where I live in Northern California. It's a great area: mountains, rivers and the nicest people. My family would love you and your wife as well, from what you have told me about her. We'd get you a good job and a top-quality house. There'd be loads of people you'd really enjoy, and I sure would like you nearby. What do you say?"

I told him thanks so much but no way. I was happy in New York and the thought of appearing in a place where I didn't know anyone didn't make any sense. He was a real nice guy, but I didn't want to leave New York.

CHAPTER 57

THE BOAT RIDE HOME

I was finally directed to a trawler, an old worn-out-looking vessel, probably used for getting supplies to and from all kinds of ships and piers. Twelve other New Yorkers and New Jerseyites were on board when it left Tokyo Harbor on the way to Manhattan.

The ship was not really equipped for us. Cots were mounted for sleeping, one over the other, on the ship's side. I recall climbing into mine, lying on my back, and only a foot over from my cot was another guy's cot. We were really squeezed in.

Eating was a riot. They gave out the food on a tray, which I took to an eating spot: a pole with a flat surface attached to it to hold the tray. The trawler bounced over the waves and wove back and forth. You ate swaying a little from side to side. After a while, I got used to it.

One night we were all awakened and told to dress rapidly and go up on deck. There, a huge rainstorm was coming down. No lightning, no thunder, just heavy rain. I went to the radio area, since I was trained in that field, to learn what was going on. The ship's Captain came by and ran to the Wheel House to direct the ship. For hours the rain came pelting down. Our ship listed from side to side, moving very slowly forward. Finally, at dawn, the storm stopped.

The Captain came to the radio room and told the operator to notify shore that we were okay. He turned to me and said, "You didn't know it, but we rocked back and forth to a great degree. If it had gotten only one degree worse, we'd have fallen over."

What luck.

As a result of the storm, our ship stalled and sat alone in the Gulf of Mexico. A plane flew over us and sent a message to the radio man: "We are looking for the S.S. Carter Braxton." Our radio man wired back, "We are the Carter Braxton, and we can't move. Our motors died in the storm."

A while later, a large ship showed up, threw ropes to our ship, and pulled it slowly until we saw the shoreline. A sailor told me, "That's Mobile, Alabama."

CHAPTER 58

MOBILE, ALABAMA

Our boat was pulled into Mobile, Alabama on December 23rd. As we walked down the gangplank to shore, I heard a very loud band playing military music. It seems the city had been alerted to our arrival. A huge crowd applauded and cheered us. The Mayor and a bunch of dignitaries stepped onto the pier, warmly welcomed us, and put garlands of flowers around our necks. Then they waved us towards limousines, which took us to City Hall.

There, two very pretty women each took one of my arms and escorted me to various parts of the city, explaining their origins and present uses. They made me feel as if I really knew their lovely city. We were then taken to an expensive restaurant for lunch, and then finally back to City Hall.

We were sent to a local camp, where we all phoned our loved ones, who so wanted us home for Christmas (including Jewish families like mine). The thirteen New Yorkers and New Jerseyites among us held a meeting, and asked for the Commanding Officer. A one-star General showed up. Our spokesman explained to him how our boat trip from Japan to the US had taken two months instead of two weeks, and asked if we could get passes to reach our home towns in time for Christmas.

The General shook his head. "No way, men," he told us.

"Okay then," our spokesman said, "we are all going AWOL so we can get home."

This General looked shocked. "Hold on for a while, let me see what I can do." And he left.

Fifteen minutes later, a young Catholic priest came in, heard our complaint, and said he'd see what was available. When he returned half an hour later, he had a big smile on his face. He told us that he'd arranged for the railroad to add a special car just for us — and that and we would be aboard in an hour, on our way to New York City.

We journeyed from Mobile to Manhattan all night. And on December 24th at 10 a.m., we arrived in New York City on 7th Avenue and 34th Street.

That's when I wandered over to my dad's company at 35th Street to start my new life as a civilian.

CHAPTER 59

MY DAD

My dad worked as a sewing machine operator for a firm called Weissman Co., on 35th Street and 7th Avenue, where he had worked since before I was drafted. Being a dedicated Communist, he was the union-dues collector. So after leaving the train at Penn Station, I walked over to the large building where Weissman was and looked in the directory. The firm was listed on the fifth floor. I took the elevator, got off on the fifth floor, and entered a huge room. It had row after row of people lined up leaning over sewing machines. The air was full of white cotton fluff, and the noise was loud.

I could see my dad in the center of one of the rows, so I tapped the shoulder of a man who was at the beginning of the row and said, "Irving," pointing in. He tapped the man next to him and so on, until my dad looked up and saw me. "My son!" he shouted, and pushed his way through the aisle until he got to me. My father hugged me close, held on to me, and cried. All the noisy sewing machines slowly cut off.

"How are you, my son?" he asked.

"Fine, Pop, I just came into New York, free as a bird."

"Oh, I'm so happy to see you." He pointed to me and cried out, "My boychick just got in from the Army." Everyone applauded. Some shouted.

Then three men strode into the room from a small hallway. One asked my dad, "Irving, this is your son, the soldier?"

"Yes, Mr. Weissman, he just arrived."

Weissman put up his hands and shouted, "Everyone — we're bringing out the whiskey to celebrate Irving's son." And two guys hastened back and came out with paper cups so we could drink and talk. I told different people whatever they asked about. Finally, I turned to Pop and said, "I have to get to the Bronx to see my wife, Pauline." When I picked up my green canvas bag, he brushed my hands off it and said he would bring it to his house and deliver it to me tomorrow. I kissed Pop and walked to the 34th Street subway station.

After my wife and I greeted each other and took such pleasure in being together, it was about 8 o'clock at night. The phone rang and it was my dad's wife, Rae. "Ebbie, where's your father?" she asked. "He's usually home by 6."

"Gee, Rae, I have no idea. Call me when he gets in."

At 8:30, Rae phoned. "Your dad's okay. He got drunk, took the wrong subway, got lost, and finally found his way home."

CHAPTER 60

EARLY CIVILIAN LIFE

When I got home to my wife in the Bronx (she was living with her mother), we immediately had sex, but that was the only time we had sex until years later when she wanted to have a baby. Then we talked a bit and ate something. After that, I told her I had to go see my grandmother, who lived only a few blocks away.

When I arrived at my grandmother's building, I hurried up to the third floor and knocked on her door. I came into her apartment and there she was — but when I went to hug her, she backed up and acted like she didn't know me. When I looked at her face, I saw that she had changed and become hardened, and didn't look like my grandmother anymore. After all, three years had passed since we had said goodbye.

Let me remind you of the circumstances of my early life. My mother, Anja, had died the first week of my life. As a consequence, my dad became morose and distant, so his mother had raised me. She did absolutely everything a loving, caring, concerned mother would do. In fact, I grew up believing that she actually *was* my mother. But as I got older and visited my friends' houses, I became aware of how much younger their mothers were. Then I started to notice how my father and my Aunt Bella called my grandmother "Mom." I wondered how she could also be *my* mom. I finally figured it out, wised up, and began to call her "Bubbe" (the Jewish word for "Grandma").

My grandmother fed me, clothed me, took me to kindergarten, my doctors' appointments, and once to the dentist. The dentist looked in my mouth, probed me with a sharp instrument, and I cried out in pain. In from the waiting room rushed my Bubbe, punched the dentist in the chest, grabbed me out of the dental chair, and brought me home. How *dare* he hurt Bubbe's little boy!

My Bubbe and I took bus rides all over New York. We went to the Jewish theater, the movies, and to Jewish delicatessens, where I ate tongue, if you can believe that. I loved everything about her. I could go on and on. Maybe one day, I'll write about the two of us.

So now, entering the Bronx apartment where I had lived with her for nineteen years, I sat down on the couch and she sat opposite me on an easy chair. There was so much I wanted to tell her. I spoke for a while, but she didn't answer. I tried again: no response.

Then it dawned on me that, from the moment I had begun speaking as a child, I had spoken to her in Yiddish. Even as I began to be trained to be an American youngster, I still always had command of basic Yiddish words to use with her. But now, after three years as a soldier, I remembered virtually nothing. No Yiddish. Blank. So I sat there and stared at her and she stared back at me. No sound. Nothing.

A half hour passed.

I left, and I never saw her again. There was no connection between us, and we didn't really know each other anymore. It was very sad.

That was the cost of the war to me. This is my very saddest memory of the war years. I weep often thinking of her, my lost, precious Bubbe.

CHAPTER 61

MEMORIES OF SOLDIERS PAST

After the war, after many years had passed, maybe twenty-five, one day I mused, "Why not just phone them, see what's up. Call Vic and Bernie, two army friends from the Bronx." So I did.

Vic's son was a young man now. He told me how his father had died only a few months before.

Bernie's wife, it turned out, was packing up and moving south to Florida. Bernie too was gone, as of the year before. It was his son who gave me this sad information.

Why hadn't I tried contacting them earlier? I knew where they lived, and initially we'd met a few times to recall our army memories, but then we had slowly lost touch. Actually, they could not have reached me if they'd tried. My work had taken me far, far away from New York to Los Angeles.

How embedded both of these friends are in my heart. I miss them. So long, Vic. Goodbye, Bernie.

Thinking back, the people I personally knew who died in my war were:

- **Levin.** Met him at lunch in a mess hall, a friend of Boyo's back in Scott Field, Illinois. Levin had completed gunner training and would be in a bomber soon, overseas somewhere. A year later, in a letter from Boyo, I learned that Levin had died when his bomber crashed. A nice guy.
- **Mo and Jo.** The funniest soldiers I ever knew. While training at Scott Field, these guys, one Polish and the other Italian, would keep up a conversation that had us all laughing. They made faces, used wild expressions, and simply amused all of us. Sadly, they both died in their bombers. I was so deeply touched when I was told.
- **"Tarzan."** Locally, there were two friends who had died in the war. One was known to me because we played ball together. In the Bronx, each street had teams playing stickball, touch football, field hockey, and basketball. My team, the 172nd Street team, would also play on adjoining streets, such as Charlotte Street. One street leader was a clean-cut, lean, dark-haired young man who we all referred to as "Tarzan." He played only the difficult positions, like shortstop or tackle. He was quite firm, but led his team with confidence and ease. I always admired him. He died in battle.
- **Abe Kupperwasser.** Last was a schoolmate of mine from the ages of six to twelve, Abe Kupperwasser. He had a German accent, having arrived in the U.S. before school age. He was pleasant to have around. He tried to fit in and although we were a tiny bit aware of his accent, we all liked Abe. He died on a boat crossing the Atlantic, sunk by a Nazi sub.

All these men remain clearly in my mind some seventy-five years after they perished. Go figure that out.

Here's a list of soldiers I knew whom I have not mentioned before. I'm mentioning them now, in case other folks reading this recognize them:

- **Ernie Rackmil.** A fraternity brother at NYU, also at a post near mine in Miami Beach, Florida, where I took basic training.
- **Jack Dolberg.** Also at training. I bumped into him later on at a clothing store where he clerked.
- **Max Scher.** From Bloomington, NY.
- **Torn Fears.** From Joplin, MO.
- **Bill Perry.** From Perry, VA.
- **Louis Gussin.** From Vermont.
- **Joe Dowling.** Also from Vermont.
- **Larry Ackert.** From Minnesota.
- **Harry Glatter**, From the Bronx, NY.
- **Ed Miller.** From Manhattan, NY.
- **Manny Cohen.** From Long Island, NY.
- **Lenny Joseph.** From Miami Beach, FL.
- **Jake Ellman.** From Long Island, NY.

They each played a meaningful role in my life as a soldier.

SO IT'S OVER

Yes, all of these experiences are deeply impressed in my mind and in my heart. Having almost died nine times, I can only believe that, as my wife Lillian used to tell me: "Your mother is watching over you."

Momma, thank you.

www.ingramcontent.com/pod-product-compliance
Lightning Source LLC
Chambersburg PA
CBHW030556080526
44585CB00012B/390